Smart Drugs, Attention Doping, and Screen Addicts

Also Available from Bloomsbury

The Disaster of Resilience: Education, Digital Privatization, and Profiteering, Kenneth J. Saltman
Race, Politics and Pandemic Pedagogy, Henry A. Giroux
Pedagogy of Resistance, Henry A. Giroux
Insurrections, Henry A. Giroux
On Critical Pedagogy, 2nd edition, Henry A. Giroux
Give Children the Vote, John Wall
Education, Equality and Justice in the New Normal, edited by Inny Accioly and Donaldo Macedo

Smart Drugs, Attention Doping, and Screen Addicts

The Drug Attention Industrial Complex in Education

Kenneth J. Saltman

BLOOMSBURY ACADEMIC
LONDON • NEW YORK • OXFORD • NEW DELHI • SYDNEY

BLOOMSBURY ACADEMIC
Bloomsbury Publishing Plc
50 Bedford Square, London, WC1B 3DP, UK
1385 Broadway, New York, NY 10018, USA
29 Earlsfort Terrace, Dublin 2, Ireland

BLOOMSBURY, BLOOMSBURY ACADEMIC and the Diana logo
are trademarks of Bloomsbury Publishing Plc

First published in Great Britain 2025

Copyright © Kenneth J. Saltman, 2025

Kenneth J. Saltman has asserted his right under the Copyright, Designs and
Patents Act, 1988, to be identified as Author of this work.

For legal purposes the Acknowledgments on p. vi constitute
an extension of this copyright page.

Cover Design by Studio Auto
Cover image © Connect Images via Getty Images

All rights reserved. No part of this publication may be reproduced or transmitted
in any form or by any means, electronic or mechanical, including photocopying,
recording, or any information storage or retrieval system, without prior
permission in writing from the publishers.

Bloomsbury Publishing Plc does not have any control over, or responsibility for,
any third-party websites referred to or in this book. All internet addresses given
in this book were correct at the time of going to press. The author and publisher
regret any inconvenience caused if addresses have changed or sites have ceased
to exist, but can accept no responsibility for any such changes.

A catalogue record for this book is available from the British Library.

A catalog record for this book is available from the Library of Congress.

ISBN: HB: 978-1-3504-4000-5
PB: 978-1-3504-3999-3
ePDF: 978-1-3504-4002-9
eBook: 978-1-3504-4001-2

Typeset by Integra Software Services Pvt. Ltd.
Printed and bound in Great Britain

To find out more about our authors and books visit www.bloomsbury.com
and sign up for our newsletters.

Contents

Acknowledgments	vi
1 Smart Drugs: The Educational Trade in Attention	1
2 Screen Addicts	31
3 Raging Hormones: Transgender Youth and the Ideology of Competition	53
4 Trauma Doping: Anti-Anxiety Medication and the New Trauma Education Industries	77
5 Race, Drugs, and the School to Prison Pipeline	99
Conclusion: Enchanting Education for Democratic Affect or Getting Kids Hooked on Theory	118
Notes	125
Index	141

Acknowledgments

Conversations with a number of friends, colleagues, and students valuably informed this project. I am grateful to all. I am tremendously appreciative of Robin Goodman who engaged with me over the entirety of the manuscript providing valuable insight and feedback, forcing me to rethink certain assumptions, and closely reading all of the chapters. I cannot thank her enough.

Bloomsbury acquisition editor Mark Richardson worked with me on the initial development of the project and I am tremendously grateful for his thoughtfulness and support.

Special thanks to Henry Giroux whose scholarship, mentorship, and friendship have played a defining role in this project and all my work.

I would like to thank my colleagues and administrators in the College of Education and Department of Educational Policy Studies at the University of Illinois Chicago for creating a supportive and collegial environment for scholarship and teaching. In particular, thanks to Dean Kathryn Chval and Chair Mark Giles.

A number of friends, colleagues, and family members provided me with unique insights into various aspects of the topics covered by this book. Special thanks to Alex Means, Noah Gelfand, Kevin Bunka, Rob Isaacs, Chris Murray, Al Lingis, Donaldo Macedo, Graham Slater, Enora Brown, Jeffrey Di Leo, Nicole Simek, Zahi Zalloua, Ourania Filippakou, Hugo Rodridguez, Josh Shepperd, Chris Murray, Mark Garrison, Rick Ohanesian, Sally Ohanesian, Michelle Decker, Abby Decker, Mary Szybist, Bob Szybist, Kathy Szybist, and Simone Saltman.

1

Smart Drugs: The Educational Trade in Attention

Introduction

Drugs are at the center of the most significant transformations of schooling. For the past two decades, with the dominance of the standards and accountability movement and business models of school reform, children have been drugged to compete on standardized tests, for greater attention in school, and have been diagnosed with Attention Deficit Hyperactivity Disorder (ADHD) at exponentially increasing rates. As screens have become ubiquitous for kids both in and out of schools, crises of "attention deficit" have expanded. Pharmaceutical stimulant solutions and digital technology products in resilience at the ready to be used against screen addiction. As trans athletes have reached greater prominence and inclusion in school sports, they and their hormones have become the targets of campaigns of hate by the political right. As diagnoses of anxiety and trauma among youth have reached epidemic proportions, prescriptions for anti-anxiety drugs have reached new highs. And as illicit drugs go mainstream and are legalized, illegal drugs remain at the center of the targeting of Black and brown youth by the juvenile justice school to prison pipeline. What these examples have in common are vast interlocked drug and attention industries in commercializing and producing youth problems for profit. Each of the five chapters details the material stakes in the education drugs attention complex: educational profiteering through the mutually supportive sales of drugs and testing products, drugs and digital screen technologies, drugs and trauma/ resilience programs, and drugs and juvenile justice services.

The contest for students' attention, consciousness, and bodies needs to be understood as part of the global agenda of the transnational capitalist class to produce differentiated workers, to contain surplus labor through technologies of control, and to depoliticize the potentially explosive class relations of an economic and educational system that depends upon increasing repression.[1] This contest involves the ways that pharma and digital technologies work in relation to each other to manage biological and psychological stimulation and excitation, banality, and drudgery, producing "enchantments" and "disenchantments" with lived experience. These chapters also explore the ideological aspects of the drug-attention complex by detailing the concepts, narratives, and representations that create the needs these industries fill and the selves these practices create. The book situates the drug attention education complex in terms of broader global economic, political, and cultural tendencies and antagonisms and provides an alternative direction for critical and democratic educational practices.

Conditions for the Drug Attention Education Complex

The drug attention education complex developed from neoliberal educational restructuring and the standards and accountability movement which was integral to it. In 2000, following heavy lobbying from test and educational publishing companies, particularly educational publisher McGraw-Hill, the United States passed federal education legislation that nationalized high-stakes standardized testing through the No Child Left Behind Law (NCLB) that reauthorized the Elementary and Secondary Education Act (ESEA).[2] Originally, the 1965 ESEA put in place federal compensatory funding for poor schools. The "high stakes" of the 2000 NCLB made federal funding dependent upon standardized test scores. NCLB marked a major implementation of the standards and accountability movement that framed school improvement through the standardization of curriculum, the alleged quantification of learning through standardized testing, and the application of disciplinary sanctions on teachers, schools, and students that do not continually reach higher and higher test scores.

The standards and accountability movement denied the politics of knowledge, the value of social context and student experience in the process of learning, and the possibilities of knowledge as instrument for social and political agency. In contrast, the standards and accountability movement framed quantified learning outcomes as a means to academic and ultimately economic rewards. The result of NCLB was that schools that did not continuously improve test scores would be financially punished and subject to potential closure. Described by critics as a punishment of the poor and an attack on schools in poor communities that had suffered historical disinvestment, NCLB would have, if continued as authorized, declared as "failed" a majority of US schools.

NCLB came at a time of the growing corporate school reform movement that promoted closure of traditional public schools and their replacement with school privatizations in the form of privately managed and sometimes for-profit charter schools, vouchers for private and religious schools, scholarship tax credits (tax incentives to opt out of public schools and use private schools), urban portfolio districts (schemes to expand privately managed and for-profit charter schools), and expanded corporate culture to pedagogy, curriculum, and administration.[3] The corporate school reform movement framed schools as needing to be treated "like businesses" and be "allowed to fail" if they did not adequately "compete" with other schools in a district. So a major dimension of NCLB would be to set up for failure-declaration a vast number of public schools that would then be subject to corporate school reform and its neoliberal prescription of closure and privatization.[4]

The convergence of the standards and accountability and corporate school reform movements meant not only disinvestment of the schools most in need of investment. It also meant massive profits for the corporations that promoted them.

> Only days after the 2000 election, an executive for publishing giant NCS Pearson addressed a Waldorf ballroom filled with Wall Street analysts. According to *Education Week*, the executive displayed a quote from President-elect [George W.] Bush calling for state testing and school-by-school report cards, and announced, "This almost reads like our business plan." The bill has allotted $387 million to get states up to speed; the National Association of State Boards of Education estimates that properly funding the testing mandate could cost anywhere from $2.7 billion to $7 billion.[5]

The educational test and textbook publishing industry promoted the standards and accountability movement, seeing the massive profit potential in their products becoming required by the new directions of federal and state laws. McGraw-Hill, Educational Testing Service [ETS], Kaplan, Houghton-Mifflin, and Pearson NCS would spend millions of dollars lobbying for decades of test-based accountability and standardization and would realize billions of dollars in profits.[6]

The numerous for-profit corporations in the corporate school reform movement represent a vast money grab of what the business press had by the 1990s framed as hundreds of millions of dollars a year in public spending taken by the private sector. For example, Educational Management Organizations ran charter schools for profit and captured public tax money that would otherwise have been spent on public school resources, salaries, and other materials for owner profits.⁷ Vast profits were secured through school commercialism, charter school real estate boondoggles, for-profit private schooling supported through vouchers, and social impact bond schemes. School commercialism allows business to advertise products like junk food and clothing to a captive audience in textbooks, on scoreboards, and through faux news programs. Charter schools enable the management of public schools for profit and lucrative administrative fee-taking by "non-profits." Charter school real estate schemes involve businesses getting school buildings for free and then charging rent to the districts who gave them as well as profit through tax credits. Voucher schemes allow business to collect per pupil funds from the public and then cut costs on educational services to maximize profit. Social Impact Bond schemes facilitate investment banks like Goldman Sachs to finance social services and double their money at public expense, cherry picking for investments already proven "successful" services under a guise of "accountability."⁸ More recently, the same players involved in promoting and financially investing in charter expansion, such as venture philanthropies and investment firms like New Schools Venture Fund and Leap Innovations, have invested in the expansion of digital educational privatizations.⁹ For-profit companies run cyber schools (such as K12, Inc), score lucrative contracts for digital Social and Emotional Learning (SEL) services in often-dubious mindfulness, meditation, and growth mindset programs as well as new AI direct reading instruction programs and biometric pedagogy programs.¹⁰

At the turn of the millennium, in the context of high-stakes standardized testing and the looming threat to public schools of being declared failed, closed, and replaced with privately managed schools under NCLB, another corporate sector was able to vastly expand. Pharmaceutical companies such as the makers of Adderall (Teva), Ritalin (Ciba now Novartis), and Vivanse (Shire now Takeda) began marketing their attention and focus drugs for the treatment of ADHD [Attention Deficit Hyperactive Disorder] to doctors, teachers, administrators, and parents.[11] In 2000, just as NCLB became law, these pharmaceutical companies released advertisements promising student success in educational competition. Investors and ideologues were promoting neoliberal ideology in education. Neoliberalism suggested that education should serve primarily market needs and that schools should be seen as businesses, students and parents as education consumers, educational administrators as corporate CEOs. Neoliberal education reformers contended that individual academic competition amongst schools and students, paired with consumer choice in educational markets, would result in individual future economic opportunities. Spurred by aggressive marketing by pharmaceutical companies and parental and student fears of adverse academic consequences of high-stakes testing and a culture of cutthroat academic competition, diagnoses of ADHD and prescriptions for attention and focus drugs exponentially increased rapidly. As Alan Schwarz points out, the American Psychological Association's estimation of a 5 percent incidence of ADHD among youth is a fraction of the diagnoses which have reached 20 percent of the youth population and in some US states reached 30 percent of boys.[12] In addition, large numbers of students from elementary school through university are sharing other students' ADHD medications and buying them illicitly so these students can medicate themselves into academic competition by pharmaceutically boosting their focus and attention.[13] Hence, the actual rates of both prescribed and non-prescribed use significantly exceed these very high official numbers.

Neoliberal education reformers not only reframed education for individual economic competition and framed education instrumentally for the economy.[14] They also discounted the humanistic and civic roles that schooling plays in preparing socially engaged citizens and stewards of the public sphere and planet. They positioned predominantly white professional-class students as principally needing to be entrepreneurial subjects of capacity who could use whatever means necessary to compete for tests and grades. In this context, Adderall and other amphetamine drugs provide students with the attention and focus tools of body self-management. The same diagnoses and drugs were also used in working-class contexts, such as predominantly Black and brown cities and predominantly white rural areas, to drug children into docility. Administrators and teachers sought to have students put on ADHD drugs to prevent them from disrupting other students' standardized test performance. Under NCLB's high-stakes punishment failure by a school to continually raise standardized test scores would result in potential financial penalties. This punitive regime that targeted financial cuts to the historically worst-funded schools, incentivized administrators and teachers to use every means at their disposal to increase test scores from transforming teaching into test preparation to manipulating the scores to drugging children.

By 2010, public discourse about skyrocketing rates of amphetamine prescription for ADHD largely focused on two problems: (1) potential health dangers such as cardiovascular risks and psychological effects of abuse such as psychosis and dependency, and (2) worries of unfair educational competition.[15] The former problem appears to be very real with high-profile stories of amphetamine addiction, abuse, mental illness, and suicide.[16] In fact, the abuse of and addiction to amphetamines following heavy marketing by pharmaceutical companies appear to parallel the opioid epidemic in the way that these companies portray potentially dangerous and addictive drugs as harmless and healthy instruments to optimize unrealized academic potential while aggressively marketing the radical expansion of prescriptions.[17]

Worries of unfair educational competition amongst users appear to have been patterned on stories about unfair and illegal use of steroids in sports such as baseball, cycling, and the Olympics. These stories simultaneously naturalized exclusionary and quantifiable educational competition by likening mental states to physical capacity and affirmed neoliberal educational ideological framing that made individual market competition and consumer choice central educational values. The concern with drugs providing an "unfair edge" obscured the extent to which standardized testing, the standardization of curriculum, the emphasis on learning facts, and repressive pedagogical approaches undermined public and critical forms of teaching and learning. Critical education makes schooling meaningful and relevant, relates learning to broader relations of power and authority, and positions knowledge as a tool for social- and self-understanding and social intervention into public problems.[18] The public discourse emphasis on health and competition failed to take up some of the most essential issues related to ADHD and prescriptions, namely, the questions of: how attention became the social value that it did when it did; how a problem of attention "deficit" related to social and educational priorities for work and the economy (including the competition for attention waged by the digital entertainment and education industries); how the drugging of children into educational attention relates to broader economic, political, and cultural trends, forces, and antagonisms, including the changing role of education in the social and cultural reproduction of the capitalist economy.

As neoliberal educational reforms, privatizations, testing, corporate culture, and profit-seeking by corporations drove a vast expansion of educational *drudgery* and pharma self-management in youth, screen usage by children of all ages steadily expanded. What I mean by educational drudgery is that neoliberal education reform produced meaningless, decontextualized forms of teaching, objectivistic discounting of student experience, and a denial of the relationship between learning and the world through the standardization and homogenization of the curriculum, scripted lessons, the erosion of teacher autonomy, and teaching to tests. Henry Giroux has referred to this student experience as "dead time" in schools.[19] Neoliberal education reform revived some of the worst aspects of early- and mid-twentieth-century models of Taylorism and scientific management that imported business models of industrial worker discipline, routinization, and standardization into schools.[20] These models had by the 1960s and 1970s been declining as progressive and democratic education promoted meaningful, dialogic, and socially relevant approaches to teaching and curriculum.

Pharmaceutical stimulants allow focus and attention, in part, by reinvesting a student experience of school drudgery with biological stimulation. Such biological stimulation replaces pedagogical stimulation that would be driven by interesting, meaningful curriculum that would motivate students with knowledge of self and social understanding, curiosity about difference and the unknown, and political agency. Put differently, in the absence of relevant, meaningful, and critical forms of teaching and learning that position knowledge as an instrument for individual and social transformation, biological stimulation serves as a motivator aiding in docility, obedient self-control in the service of what Freire called "banking education."[21] Banking education wrongly presumes that students are empty vessels to be filled with knowledge, that knowledge is a static thing like a commodity, that teachers are delivery agents rather than intellectuals, and that learning is a process of knowledge consumption rather than a dialogic exchange between teachers and students. Pedagogies of corporeal control furthered by pharma and screens expand at the expense of critical pedagogies that make education an instrument of self and social comprehension, a means of political agency, and a venue for expanding democratic social relations throughout society.

What is at stake in the convergence of the testing, school privatization, and pharmaceutical industries is more than the case of several industries targeting public schools, students, and parents to extract profit. While that is a major part of this story, it would be myopic to comprehend the problem as nothing more than a kind of corporate conspiracy by powerful monied actors. As Stuart Hall pointed out, such framing misses the broader social dynamic and interplay of, on the one hand, broader social forces such as capitalism and, on the other hand, subjectivity and agency which are formed and informed by social forces but also constitute society and struggle to remake it.[22] The contemporary battle for attention and its capture through pharmaceutical or screen technologies needs to be situated in terms of antagonisms over broader societal forces and structures, the extents to which cultural practices such as schooling reproduce these forces and structures, but also ethical-political and ideological antagonisms and discursive pedagogical constitution of subjectivity through cultural meaning-making practices. Thinking of the contests over attention in this way it becomes necessary to consider attention a social and historical construction that is a site and stake of political contestation, material control, and forms of consciousness.

In the 2000s, just as test-based accountability, the application of market-style pressures, and amphetamine usage were growing, so too was student use of digital devices and screens. Screen use has long been correlated with ADHD symptoms and diagnosis, and the amount of screen usage correlates with the severity of symptoms.[23] More generally, screen use simultaneously positions subjects as both passive recipients of information, narrative, signs, and ideologies. Screen use, simultaneously, invests experience with heightened sensual titillation. Screen use habituates individuals to passively consume rather than actively engage with the knowledge, assertions, narratives, and ideologies of others.[24] Screen use also renders everyday experience dull, banal, depressing, and lacking the incessant stimulation of fireball explosions and shootings of action films and television, sexualized enticements of advertisements, emoji approvals of texts, chiming behaviorism of games and gamified learning apps, choreographed pop music, hatred, and clickbait headlines of social media. While some people, some of the time, do read against the grain of, resist, and critically interrogate what they watch, the speed, quantity, and prevalence of media flows overwhelm and by some accounts sicken subjectivity.[25] Thirty years ago Jonathan Crary recognized the relationship between digital screen technology and its production of inattention in youth and the efforts to manage youth bodies through other means. He is worth quoting at length here:

> Clearly, many of the systemic measures in place now for the efficient management of attention are working imperfectly at best. Many of the modes of fixation, of sedentarization, of enforced attentiveness implicit in the diffusion of the personal computer may have achieved some of its disciplinary goals, in the production of what Foucault calls docile bodies. The proliferation of electronic and communication products insures that docility will always be linked with intensified patterns of consumption, but the forms of social disintegration that have accompanied this new regime have generated behaviors (e.g. children who will not learn) that have become systematically intolerable. And, as the institutional discourse on attention indicates, we are now seeing the dramatic expansion of another layer of disciplinary technology—the sweeping use of potent neurochemicals as a strategy of behavior management.[26]

The management of behavior that Crary wrote of includes the use of drugs in schools to artificially induce attention, endure drudgery, pacify, and make productive. The use of pharma stimulation attached to learning can be comprehended analogously to the widespread use of stimulants to endure the drudgery of work. From the chewing of coca leaves in the Andes of South America to aid in the endurance of hard, cold, repetitive, physical labor to the chewing of betel nut in Asia for the same and the office coffee break, stimulants in relatively low dosage have long been used to add stimulation, elevation, and feelings of well-being to contexts that are banal, dull, and repetitive.

Drugging children into attention and focus is centrally related to the problem of meaning, interest, and learning for agency. In other words, the framing of an "attention deficit" as an educational and medical problem obscures the crucial question of *what is worth paying attention to* for students. However, the dominant discourses about ADHD, pharmaceutical treatment of it, their uses in education, and the relationship of screen time to the problems of attention all largely efface both the problems of meaningful learning and interest. The dominant framing also conceals how it is that attention becomes a social problem for some people at some times, as well as the converging of several industries that synergistically extract profit from the management of youth bodies and the sales of products to the public, schools, and parents. What is at stake in comprehending and challenging in the Drug-Attention-Industrial-Complex is the possibility of expanding critical and democratic forms of education that make learning relevant, meaningful, socially critical, and socially transformative. At a historical moment when egalitarian, democratic, and humanistic values are in the crosshairs of autocratic and fascist movements around the world, the imperative could not be greater for education to be recognized for its role in cultivating global democratic cultures, public institutions of care, and educative sites that foster critical consciousness and the capacities for engaged, collective, self-governance.[27]

Drugging children into attention for meaningless, decontextualized, allegedly neutral, and objective educational content works similarly to the digital gamification of knowledge or "edutainment." These banking education approaches entertain for the consumption of fact and discreet skill. For example, math games have students solving basic equations to enable an avatar to shoot lasers to kill space aliens. The sounds and sights of the video game link sensory stimulation to an otherwise boring and socially decontextualized approach to learning math skills. Likewise, language learning apps teach language using behaviorist chimes, points, and a competition with other learners, but they do not teach the language in a way that connects it to student experience, the social context, or the broader social world. These apps approach learning as a discreet skill and the lessons are homogenized, standardized, and intended to be universal. Hence, they are framed as apolitical, having no relation to actual cultural contexts or social antagonisms. Even as these gamified learning programs misrepresent their content as apolitical and non-ideological, just a skill, the gamified form produces a cultural pedagogy of consumerism in which knowledge is positioned as in the service of entertainment.

Of course, there are also political and ideological dimensions of delinking mathematics education from the broader social context and what Adorno referred to as "the essentially real."[28] Some of what is "essentially real" are "the laws of motion of society, especially the laws which express how the present situation has come into being and where it is tending to go."[29] The teaching of math, as a discreet supposedly objective neutral skill used by the student to accumulate facts, presumes that there are no politics or ethical implications for existing social institutions such as the scientific, engineering, and business purposes of the finance or weapons industries. Adorno writes, "[T]he world of facts has degenerated into a cloak, a veil that conceals what is essentially real."[30] There are decidedly different ethical and political implications of learning math to comprehend and intervene in public problems. For example, critical mathematics education teaches mathematics skills through the identification of public problems, and the skill helps in further understanding and analyzing the problem as well as developing projects to address it. A teacher in a Chicago middle school teaches students in a predominantly non-white school to use percentages and decimals to analyze racist police "driving while black/brown" disparate rates of pullovers.[31] The mathematics skills gained through dialog with the teacher allow students to better comprehend the discrimination, and the lesson involves strategizing for how to publicize the information to collectively counter the problem.[32] In this case the new knowledge becomes the basis for students to see learning as a source of agency and potential social transformation. Similarly, critical mathematics can teach math skills to analyze and criticize radically increasing rates of ADHD diagnoses and prescriptions, help students investigate the causes, and develop projects that promote meaningful and critical forms of pedagogy over pedagogies of control.

Several explanatory paradigms interpret the rise of ADHD diagnosis and prescription. First, there is an empiricist approach that relies upon scientific studies of attention, drugs, and screentime impact. While this approach provides insights into the extent to which ADHD diagnosis and drug prescription are driven more by profit-seeking than science, the framing of the problems takes for granted the troubling conception of "attention deficit" and fails to comprehend the social and cultural construction of attention imperatives. As a consequence, the empiricist approach naturalizes as beyond question what are in fact political contests over attention, attention drugs, digital attention capture technologies, and the extents to which such contests are waged through schools, concealing broader social antagonisms.

Second, some critical perspectives on attention situate the rise of ADHD diagnosis and drug prescription within the broader transformations of contemporary capitalism, the struggles over subjectivity, the body and its attention within structural dynamics. Some critical perspectives on attention such as Franco Berardi's are grounded in materialist conceptions of society and subjectivity. These provide distinct insights about the body as contested terrain for attention capture in semio-capitalism. Berardi explains how the industrial capitalist crises of overproduction are cyclical while in semio-capitalism crisis becomes permanent,

As semio-capitalism is based on the constant exploitation of mental energy, and competition constitutes the general form of relations in the precarious labor market, mental suffering has become a social epidemic. The main source of pathology is competition in the area of interpersonal relations. The individual symptoms of this epidemic are the constant stress on attention, the reduction of the time available for affection, loneliness, existential misery, then angst, panic, and depression. In this way, psychopathology and economics are increasingly linked. In the transition to semiocapitalism, mental suffering no longer concerns a small minority of weird people, but tends to become the norm in a system that is based on the exploitation of precarious cognitive work.[33]

Materialist perspectives such as Berardi's, as valuable as they are, make it difficult to retain a focus on how attention is dependent upon meaning and how the struggle over attention is about not just the struggle over the body and relations of force but also the struggle over consciousness and the possibilities in fostering critical consciousness. It is necessary to emphasize how the technologies of attention capture that aim to control the body come at the expense of critical forms of education that provide self and social understanding and agency for social intervention.

Drugging Children into Attention

Investigative journalist Alan Schwarz wrote a series of articles for *The New York Times* as well as a book about the rise of ADHD and the financial profit-seeking driving it. Schwarz observed the radical increase in ADHD diagnoses. From 1990 to 2013, diagnoses in children went from 600,000 to 3.5 million.[34] According to contemporary data from the Center for Disease Control [CDC], 6 million children between the ages of 3 and 17 have been diagnosed with ADHD.[35] Contrary to medical industry doxa that expanding diagnoses represent a worsening of this "disease," Schwarz pointed out, "The rise of ADHD diagnoses and prescriptions for stimulants over the years coincided with a remarkably successful two-decade campaign by pharmaceutical companies to publicize the syndrome and promote the pills to doctors, educators and parents."[36] Schwarz indicates that the marketing campaign by pharma made "normal" childhood behaviors abnormal and symptoms of disease. The maker of Adderall in advertisements promoted diagnosis based on such common childhood traits as carelessness, impatience, forgetfulness, and poor grades.

Pharma advertised its drugs to parents as a solution to educational competition, "as grounds for medication that, among other benefits, can result 'in schoolwork that matches his intelligence.'"[37] This multipronged marketing approach included the use of highly remunerated sponsored physician spokespeople, fabricated patient advocacy groups, and the distribution to children of ADHD comic books intended to promote diagnosis and treatment.[38] The companies aggressively advertised directly to parents[39] and to school districts.[40]

These marketing efforts by pharmaceutical companies paid off massively as ADHD became by 2013 the second most diagnosed disease in children with resultant skyrocketing drug sales of amphetamines to children.[41] By 2012, sales of stimulant drugs for ADHD reached $9 billion per year, increasing fivefold from $1.7 billion ten years earlier. At around this time, pharmaceutical companies began to target the adult market the way they had the child market. By 2022, sales reached $12.4 billion, with projected sales expected to hit $14.8 billion by 2030.[42] Since 2000 the FDA fined the makers of all the leading stimulant ADHD drugs for false and misleading advertising, some even fined multiple times.[43]

The medical-pharmaceutical-psychiatric establishment framed ADHD as a disease that was getting the diagnosis and treatment that it deserved. Contrary to this framing, critics argue that ADHD is vastly overdiagnosed and that the overdiagnosis has largely been driven by the pursuit of pharmaceutical profit-seeking.[44] The founding figure who named and codified ADHD, Dr. Keith Conners, contended that the incidence of it is 2–3 percent in school-age children, dramatically less than the 15–30 percent rates of diagnosis.[45] In addition to the three-decades-long marketing campaign for stimulant drugs and the defining of normal childhood behaviors as symptoms, critics claim that there is no definitive test for ADHD.[46] What is more, international comparisons between nations such as the United States and the United Kingdom show radically disparate rates of diagnosis and prescription, with the United States by far leading the world.[47] Such enormous differences across contexts raise doubts about a medical-biological basis for radical increases in diagnosis and prescription.

In addition, the very same amphetamine drugs that are dominant in the treatment of ADHD were in the 1950s to 1970s sold over-the-counter in US supermarkets as diet and weight loss drugs with brand names such as Obetrol. The uses of this drug spanned appetite suppressant diet aid, work productivity tool, and recreational upper. Prior to this, amphetamine salts were used as early as the late nineteenth century as asthma treatment and in the first half of the twentieth century as a military tool by Axis and Allied armies to heighten aggression, confidence, and morale and counter fatigue from sleepless *blitzkriegs*. As these amphetamine salt-mixed compounds were regulated in the early 1970s in the United States, new purposes for them were being devised by their manufacturers.

Beyond the historical uses of amphetamine salts a more comprehensive look at the history of attention itself reveals the extent to which ADHD and the concept of "attention deficit" are only intelligible within a particular social and cultural conjuncture. This calls into question the naturalistic thesis that would provide biologically deterministic explanations for ADHD, changes in rates of diagnosis, and prescriptions for medications. In other words, it is not enough to recognize that there are material interests in the promotion of a crisis of youth inattention; it is also necessary to consider how the very concept of attention is historical, political, and cultural.

The Social and Historical Construction of Attention

In *Suspensions of Perception: Attention, Spectacle, and Modern Culture*, Jonathan Crary provides a history of modern attention. He argues that not only is attention a relatively recent social and historical construction but that it is thoroughly wrapped up with relations of power.[48] Crary points out that institutional and power struggles over attention begin in the nineteenth century.[49] Attention becomes a problem and object of concern in the context of modernized labor arrangements that produce inattention.[50] The cultural logic of industrial capital naturalizes the rapid change in attention.[51] Crary explains that attention becomes a modern problem not only due to the transformations of labor but as well through the particular form that technology has taken to form atomistic consumer subjectivity. We have inherited Thomas Edison's market vision of individualized consumers and solitary rather than collective forms of selfhood.[52] Crary contends that the cultural logic of modern capitalism produces the need for multitasking, quick changes to attention, and that contemporary culture is premised on inattention.[53] Consequently, it makes no sense to stigmatize distraction.[54]

> Over the last few years we have been reminded of the durability of attention as a normative category of institutional power, in the form of the dubious classification of an "attention deficit disorder (or ADD) as a label for unmanageable schoolchildren and others. Without entering into the larger issue of the social construction

of illness, what stands out is how attention continues to be posed as a normative and implicitly natural function whose impairment produces a range of symptoms and behaviors that variously disrupt social cohesion. One recent study on ADD declares, "What is deficient is the control exerted over behavior by rules," making explicit that the real concern is with rule-governed conduct.[55]

In the context of public schools such rule-governed conduct contributes to the ideology of social control and to the social and cultural reproduction of the stratified labor force: children need to be taught submission and obedience in order to be better workers in the future. Crary wrote this at the end of a transition from industrial to finance capital and corresponding transformations from Fordist to post-Fordist modes of self and social control.[56]

Schooling during industrial capitalism functioned to reproduce the labor force through the differential teaching of skills and know-how wrapped in class-based ideology.[57] Fordist forms of control involved time-and labor-intensive forms of learned self-discipline, setting the stage for owner profit through the short-changing of disciplined worker labor. Such time- and labor-intensive forms of social and cultural reproduction would give way in the postindustrial economy to direct corporeal coercion. Psychiatric talk therapy would give way to the management of the body and its emotions directly with pills for anxiety, depression, and attention. Criminal-justice-learned-rehabilitation through internalized disciplinary surveillance would give way to locking away bodies in solitary confinement on a vast scale. Learned self-regulation to submit to the authority of the teacher prepared students to become workers who would submit to the authority of the boss; this gave way to ramped up direct coercion of students. Direct coercion in schools took the form of repressive pedagogies, militarized and prisonized schools, biometric security and pedagogy devices, and the self-administration of pharmaceuticals to control mood, anxiety, focus, and attention. Learned self-discipline of the Fordist era was not only replaced by direct coercion but also accompanied by the new forms of control. For example, some new for-profit digital SEL apps purport to teach learned self-control while other digital apps promote behaviorist forms of direct coercion. Just a few examples include: Go Noodle and Class Dojo which involve disciplinary surveillance and lessons in learned self-control, Centervention's ZooU that purports to teach students "appropriate" social relationships by putting them alone in front of screens to interact with avatars, Amira Learning's avatar-based direct reading instruction.

Attention and Educational Repression Making the Global Labor Force, Targeting the Student Body

Global capitalism in its contemporary financialized form has specific uses for education systems. These uses include reproducing the global labor force in forms that involve prescribed skills and know-how and ideologies of social control. These racialized class-based prescriptions are implicated in reproducing the global class hierarchy. Roughly 1 percent of the population (the transnational capitalist class [TCC]) owns and controls about 80 percent of the capital; 20 percent do the managerial and knowledge work to maintain the system (transnational political elites) and 80 percent (working class) do the labor that produces value.[58] As William I. Robinson points out and as evident in documents from the World Bank and Organisation for Economic Co-operation and Development (OECD), the TCC agenda for education aims to teach the 80 percent basic skills and know-how and ideologies and dispositions of docility and submission to authority in the workplace.

The TCC agenda for the professional class (transnational political elite) 20 percent involves greater intellectual engagement and ideological indoctrination to the rules of the game including neoliberal values of competitive individualism, social Darwinist zero sum competition, and values of entrepreneurial self-management. Robinson argues that schools also prepare working-class and poor students for a future of shrinking jobs and shrinking high-skill, high-pay jobs. They do so with repression by warehousing students and preparing them for prison and to be turned into surplus labor (a significant segment of the labor force unemployed so that capitalists have the ultimate tool to discipline labor—the threat to fire).[59] Such "preparation" for the economy includes the teaching of the ideology of entrepreneurialism that prepares working-class students without capital not for starting businesses but for "flexible" work in the gig economy. As well, the growth of technologies of automation such as AI and self-driving vehicles portends a future of shrinking jobs in not just the high-tech, high-pay sector but in the service and industrial sector as well.[60] As Elon Musk recently stated to the UK prime minister, AI will produce an unprecedented future of masses of humanity whose needs can be met with technology but whose labor is unnecessary.[61] As jobs shrink, the capitalist class is faced with a choice of providing welfare state supports such as universal basic income or seeking to profit from commodified repression such as for-profit prison, private security, and privatized schools with repressive models. That is, as a growing segment of the population in financialized capitalism is redundant to production, they are filtered into institutions of commodified repression such as prison industries.

Robinson explains that the expansion of prisonized and militarized schooling as well as cultures of control in schooling is part of such industries and preparation for entry into adult institutions of control. What is more, the current crisis of surplus capital accumulation means that capital is seeking to find new investments in hitherto unseen places such as in the lifeworld and subjectivity.[62] The newest frontier in educational markets includes the turn to commodifying youth bodies, their affect and behavior through the combination of quantification and datafication and SEL digital products. For example, Lego and the OECD have promoted the quantification of play to make quantified play into a global learning standard that can be fulfilled through Lego's digital toys and education products that prescribe play with their recipe-oriented version of play, use it to market entertainment products and capture student data through the growing convergence of tablet apps and physical toys. The data itself becomes capital as children become captive data production engines.[63] This is justified through human capital discourse that claims that "non-cognitive skills" must be developed in support of cognitive skills. All of this of course takes up learning in ways that delink learning from students' cultures, contexts, and experiences and delink learning from its uses to understand and act on the world the students inhabit.

What Adderall and other attention drugs have to do with these realities is that (1) they serve as an instrument of control in the social and cultural reproduction of the racialized hierarchical labor force. As an instrument of professional-class youth to self-manage capacity for entrepreneurial subjectivity, amphetamines allow for self-disciplining and docility of the future labor force, habituating students into enduring submission to authority and the drudgery of meaningless tasks. Amphetamine stimulants are also prescribed to working-class youth as an instrument of corporeal control. (2) Pharmaceutical stimulants are one element of a broader industry in educational contracting that treats student bodies as a kind of new market frontier to commodify and commercialize student affect and behavior. This trend is evident in the OECD's efforts to quantify and create standardized tests of student affect and behavior in "non-cognitive skills" such as play.[64] It is also evident in the explosion in digital educational contracting in software and apps in social networking, SEL programs, digital mindfulness and meditation programs, and other programs that capture, quantify, and commercialize student behavior as data. Such digital educational contracting represents the growing form that educational privatization takes as it expands from the still-growing privatization of schools and their management to the privatization of the student's body.

Cannibal Capitalism and the Pathologies of the Attention Trade

In *Cannibal Capitalism,* Nancy Fraser explains that in the current era of financialized capitalism, capitalism pillages its own social and cultural reproduction functions, including by pillaging public goods and services.[65] That is, capitalism is destroying and commodifying forms of life that support capitalist production. A clear educational example of this is the privatization of public schools. Capitalism requires workers educated with the skills, know-how, and ideological dispositions for capitalist production. However, public education is being pillaged by the pursuit of new markets through, for example, destroying public schools, creating bad privatized schools with resources siphoned off by the rich, and making students into data generation engines through digital contracting, as well as a variety of swindles devoid of educational benefit but designed to enrich investors like social impact bonds, real estate charter investment boondoggles, and expensive programs in new age meditation and "social and emotional learning" that do not teach students to understand themselves or their society.[66] And while students may not learn much, they do learn that they should be "resilient," adaptable subjects who are individually responsible for their life outcomes. As Fraser points out, cannibal capitalism reaches deep inside of nature to enclose the commons of nature. This includes privatizing or enclosing the nature of our own biology, affect, and subjectivity. Some of the more glaring examples of such enclosure of subjectivity come in the form of behaviorist programs in grit pedagogy, the use of biometric pedagogy devices that teach to elicit and measure physical reactions to the teacher rather than engaging with the mind and consciousness through dialog, products, and programs that aim to quantify, datafy, and commercialize behavior and affect that aim to make student behavior and dispositions into testable standardized measures. Corporations that sell digital products, toys, and curriculum products stand to profit immensely through such projects. Such efforts control student affect toward the end of making entrepreneurial subjects, consuming subjects, "resilient" subjects, data producing subjects, and docile subjects who can be commodified for the industries of youth repression.

In her analysis of global financialized capitalism, Fraser explains that economic production depends upon labor exploitation and that labor exploitation depends upon extraction. For example, in order to produce profits, workers are exploited by paying them less than the value of their labor. The possibility of doing this depends upon uncompensated supports including, for example, the unpaid family wage or second shift of gendered domestic labor, or we could add the uncompensated labor of students learning skills, know-how, and dispositions for work. As Fraser points out, the economic dependence of exploitation on extraction depends upon racism and "externalized" environmental despoliation. The computer this is written on, the cell phones we all use, the online classroom curriculum products, the digital avatar-scripted reading programs are only possible with the use of cobalt in lithium-ion batteries. Most cobalt is extracted by superexploited workers in the Democratic Republic of Congo, many of whom are children. These workers, in brutal conditions, are exposed to dangerous toxic chemicals that pollute the local environment and contaminate the groundwater. The point not to be missed is that there is an out-of-sight and out-of-mind human and planetary cost to the educational political economy of attention that does not get recorded on balance sheets. Businesses are able to pretend that they are not harming children by making such costs invisible on their balance sheets as they commercialize the attention of youth via screens while competing to sell digital and pharmaceutical attention products to school districts, parents, and students.

As Fraser emphasizes, labor exploitation depends upon expropriation (mining, coerced labor). Capitalism makes divisions between exploitable ("First World") and expropriable (non-"First World") classes, and this division is deeply racialized.[67] For example, migrant laborers who are brown and Black work in the informal economy doing a wide array of agricultural and food processing work that makes it possible for advanced economies to eat. In education, there is a racialized three-tiered split in the workings of social and cultural reproduction. Schools educate professional-class youth for future knowledge work and management of the public and private sectors. Schools educate some working-class students for their future labor exploitation. Schools also warehouse predominantly non-white working-class and poor students in cities where containment is the primary agenda rather than skills and ideological dispositions. However, this containment is increasingly commodified in digital form as the presence of students justifies the expenditure of public money on private for-profit services in repressive pedagogy techniques, products, and programs: the purchase of surveillance technology ranging from CCTV and metal detectors to phone apps, private security to AI-scripted reading instruction, and digital SEL products. Despite being of dubious educational value, these products are of great economic value for the owners of such businesses. As they serve to transfer public and state funding to private companies, these products are not only a means for educational profiteering but they are decidedly bereft of critical and democratic pedagogical values and approaches, serving instead as instruments in a pedagogy of repression, control, and the depositing of knowledge. Such programs decidedly do not support students learning critical pedagogical values such as relating claims to truth to questions of authority, comprehending how knowledge relates to broader social and political antagonisms, interests, and ideologies, or understanding learning and knowledge as means of collective social and political interventions.

In her discussion of cannibal capitalism, Fraser identifies educational privatization as a form of capitalism destroying its own conditions of reproduction.[68] She emphasizes that capitalist predation destroys the caregiving responsibility of the public sphere in its erosion of public education. While this is true, cannibal capitalism also destroys the role of public schools in fostering critical consciousness, politically engaged forms of subjectivity, and social and political agency made possible by critical pedagogical projects that foster in students the capacities to comprehend knowledge in relation to power and authority. Schools are a site of struggle to make democratic and critical capacities by forging and teaching non-commodified values. However, cannibal capitalism does not only target schools and other public institutions in ways that undermine critical capacities; also, contemporary financialized capitalism, particularly in its digital and symbolic forms, targets subjectivity itself producing pathologies including anxiety, depression, and ADHD.

Pathologies of Semio-capitalism and Attention Economy

In a series of books including *The Soul at Work*, *Heroes*, and *And*, Franco Berardi criticizes how contemporary corporations which he dubs "semio-corporations" aim to make relations between machines and cognitive workers flexible and as a consequence are producing subjective pathology.[69] These semio-corporations as well as their digital products demand of workers and consumers multitasking which produces burnout, exhaustion, and ADHD.[70] As Berardi explains, the psychological stimulation of electronic flows leads to changes in the affective and emotional makeup of subjects, mutations to language, imagination, and the very perception of time.[71] Berardi points out that while cyberspace and its electronic flow of data, imagery, and representations can expand infinitely, cybertime, that is, our physically mediated experience of cyberspace, has corporeal and psychic limits.[72] Drugs such as amphetamines allow some degree of adaptation to the demands of cyberspace but, ultimately, no self-administered technology or pharmaceutical tool can accommodate the self to the psychic demands of a tsunami of information. For Berardi, this disjuncture between cybertime and cyberspace is producing the experience of alienation on a vast scale. For Berardi, greater drug use, not only attention and focus drugs like amphetamines but also anti-anxiety and depression drugs such as diazepines and SSRIs, manage the mental suffering, anxiety, and sadness produced by the gap between cyberspace and cybertime.[73] We can increase our efficiency through the use of pharmacology but experience cannot be intensified beyond a biological limit. Berardi emphasizes that the focus on attention and the problem of inattention is a symptom of competitive social relations in semio-capitalism. Contemporary semio-capitalism is premised on the corporate capture (by Google, Meta, etc.) of human attention which is a finite resource. The capitalist assault on attention causes a contraction of time for both emotional engagement and the rational engagement necessary for political participation.[74]

Conclusion: From the Pathologies of Capitalism to the Pedagogical Formation of Critical Consciousness

This chapter began by illustrating how the expansion of ADHD diagnosis and prescriptions for its treatment were imbricated with the standards and accountability movement and neoliberal corporate school reform movement as well as other educational and pharmaceutical profiteering initiatives. It has highlighted how the political and cultural contests over attention as concept and resource are inextricably bound to class antagonisms on a global scale. While Crary emphasizes the constructedness of attention and ADHD, Robinson and Fraser help to situate it within the social mandates of a global financialized economy that increasingly functions through coercion and pillages its own conditions of reproducibility, including education, thereby producing social and individual pathologies. Berardi emphasizes that these pathologies, which are subjectively experienced, involve the capitalist tsunami of digital information and the incapacity of the flesh to weather the digital wave. One might be tempted to come to the conclusion that structural and technological forces are determining subjective experience and foreclosing any possibility of resistance or political contestation to these destructive tendencies.

However, I want to return to a key part of my argument here to suggest that this is in fact the wrong conclusion to draw. The educational projects (behaviorist grit pedagogies, mindfulness SEL programs, digital educational products like AI reading avatars) and pharmacological products (amphetamines) that aim to amplify attention and capture attention are all premised on addressing the problem of inattention and disinterest. On the one hand the value of inattention itself cannot be discounted. Contemplation, imagination, questioning, wondering, and enchantment with the unfamiliar defy instrumental and vocational imperatives. Contemplation and imagination lead to consideration of the limitations of what is and possibility of what could be. Such wonderment lends itself to forms of education that are pleasurable, meaningful, and socially engaged. The goal must be to transform educational practices to become meaningful and socially engaged and transformative rather than drugging children into compliance to drudgery. Pedagogies of control including drugging children into attention for meaningless lessons which are rituals of obedience need to be comprehended as specifically displacing critical pedagogies that are meaningful to students and make learning and knowledge instruments for social and political intervention and control. Critical pedagogies not only make learning into the basis for social and political understanding and agency; they also accord with the values of a society theoretically committed to democratic forms of collective self-governance.

It would also be a mistake to follow those who frame digital screen culture itself as nothing more than a kind of drug and see the subjective effects of digital culture as determining of psychological states of depression, anxiety, ADHD, and alienation. Digital products cannot be bracketed off from the broader social forces that inform subjective experience such as the alienation and atomization of capitalism; nor can they be comprehended apart from the cultures and ideologies within which they become intelligible and potentially attractive. The allure of digital products is inextricably bound to social meanings. Some of the allure of digital products is the ways that they are ideologically seductive. For example, the abovementioned math video games (shooting lasers at space aliens by answering computation problems) appeal in part by affirming ideologies of competitive individualism, fantasies, and narratives of science fiction entertainment, and technological utopianism. In other words, these products decontextualize learning of math from the social possibilities of math for public and political interventions and instead ground math learning in ideological spectacle and commercial promise. Screen products also are alluring in how they simultaneously position the user in a passive spectatorial role while also stimulating the user with heightened visual and audio stimulation. Like drugs, screen products allow a form of subjective escape and withdrawal from often-unpleasant lived experience simultaneous with a form of physical stimulation. The problem of screen usage is inextricably bound up with a crisis of agency. Namely, as the next chapter discusses, screen use disenchants lived experience by mediating experience in a titillated yet passive state. The experience of reality unmediated by screens appears dull and banal but also demanding in that it requires action instead of passivity. Pharmaceutical stimulants reinvest experience with stimulation and facilitate attention and motivation. However, we must transform education to become meaningful, contextual, and socially engaged by making knowledge an instrument for social power. This promises to motivate students and render the technologies of stimulation and attention capture unnecessary, unattractive, and objects of critique.

2

Screen Addicts

On top of the technology industries that profit from getting eyeballs in front of screens, there is another industry that profits by decrying the contemporary crisis of screen addiction. The crisis of screen addiction sells advertising, click through profits, and subscriptions generated by alarming news headlines, medical websites, books, and dedicated rehab centers. "Addicted to Your Phone, Try This Calm Masterclass"—Click on the calm.com masterclass to subscribe and treat your screen addiction with yet more screentime.[1] You can be queried on your phone, tablet, TV, or laptop by CNN asking, "How Much Screentime Is Too Much? The Signs You're Addicted to Your Phone."[2] Meanwhile www.nytimes.com asks, "Is Your Child a Digital Addict?"[3] Screen addiction is not a medical or psychiatric illness classified in the Diagnostic and Statistical Manual of the American Psychological Association (DSM-IV). However, a narrower variant "video gaming disorder" or "internet gaming disorder" can be found identified as a formal illness by the World Health Organization in the eleventh edition of the International Classification of Diseases. Despite the lack of consensus on definition or symptomology, screen addiction as a public crisis and object of academic study is a term applied to people of all ages but of acute concern is its impact on children.

Prior to the Covid-19 pandemic, the American Academy of Pediatrics warned parents to limit screen time for children to less than 1 hour per day, warning of developmental damage.[4] With the onset of the pandemic, online distance-learning resulted in young children being put in front of screens all day. A widespread consensus developed during the pandemic that fully online K12 schooling was damaging and an educational failure. Despite this, students are being put in front of screens for large portions of the school day,[5] even after the pandemic. As students also use screens outside of schools at an unprecedented level, parents, teachers, and medical professionals decry "screen addiction" as threat to impulse control and self-regulation.[6]

Normalized by the pandemic, the use of screens in school has steadily expanded. Even as social media, in particular, is framed as a threat and bans on phones in schools have become more prevalent, nearly all US schools have invited social media and online applications into schools. Technology and education corporations seek to get into schools for lucrative contracts in curriculum products, automated reading and mathematics training, and SEL products or get into schools with freeware that leads into marketing for-profit services to families. The United States is not alone. Screen-based educational technology is proliferating globally. Educational technology was a $143 billion market in 2023 and is projected to reach 10 trillion by 2030.[7] In the US digital S.E.L. programs are a booming industry with powerful lobbying associations (CASEL, SEL4US, SEL Providers Association) that work to get these programs adopted and paid for by public districts, states, and the federal government. Both the businesses and the associations promoting them sponsor favorable research. Analysis of the efficacy of the programs merge sponsored with independent research, warning of business bias in the studies yet ignoring their own warnings by endorsing the programs anyway.[8] SEL screen products and programs claim to teach social skills, emotional self-awareness, character, and self-regulation.[9] That is, *the very services these products supposedly provide (self-regulation a.k.a. self-control or "executive function") are on screens, possibly contributing to a decrease in self-regulation and hence an increase in distraction and attention deficit* (as well as depression and loneliness), according to medical and scientific empirical research.[10] Hence, digital educational products appear to produce the very disorder they seek to remedy while also potentially fueling demand for attention drugs.

The discourse of screen addiction is the flip side of the constructed crisis of inattention that educational products (SEL, mindfulness, growth mindset apps) in self-regulation and stimulant drugs aim to remedy. While the crisis of attention deficit fosters worries that a student will not consume prescribed knowledge, the crisis of screen addiction fosters worries that the student will consume too much of the wrong knowledge: YouTube videos, online games, social media. The crisis of screen addiction also expresses fears that the use of screen technology will cause a decline or failure of development of "executive function," that is, self-control in children. This demanded self-control is framed as necessary for consumption of prescribed knowledge in a positivist system of "banking education."[11] Hence, in a neoliberal educational environment and a society that equates learning with earning (as opposed to better roles for learning discussed below), the alleged danger of screen use to a student's self-discipline to obediently consume prescribed knowledge implies a threat not just to students' academic futures but their material futures.

This chapter argues that screen addiction among youth and adults *is* a problem but not for the reasons that are popularized and commercialized. The dominant narrative about screen addiction frames digital technology as akin to an addictive drug that overtakes and controls the subject. It frames the problem of screen addiction for youth as a threat to obedience, discipline, and self-control, particularly endangering students' proper consumption of knowledge. On the contrary, I contend that the problem of screen addiction needs to be understood as a broader problem with and expression of contemporary capitalism that produces disenchantment, alienation, commodified subjectivity, meaninglessness, and the banalization of non-screen experience—all of which drive screen addiction. Like "attention deficit," the dominant framing of the problem of screen addiction actively denies what it is that attracts attention—that which is meaningful and stimulating. This chapter argues that in the context of education, the crisis of screen addiction participates in framing learning as a matter of discipline and obedience for the consumption of official knowledge rather than comprehending learning in terms of interest, meaning, enchantment, and agency. Hence, the crisis of screen addiction participates in affirming and promoting conceptions of schooling and learning that are about obedience rather than thinking, conformity rather than critical engagement, and learning as an exercise in meaningless drudgery (bolstered by an empty commercial promise) rather than learning as a catalyst to social understanding and power.

The first section considers how screen-use produces disenchantment in the form of alienation, consumerist and conformist forms of agency and commodified subjectivity rather than public, democratic, and critical forms of agency. It develops my argument from the first chapter that the passive stimulation of screens banalizes non-screen experience that then requires pharma stimulation to endure a disenchanted off-screen reality, or it requires yet more screen time—hence screen addiction. The second section details the ways that educational technologies of attention control such as for-profit digital educational products in resilience (SEL, mindfulness) fail to address the conditions that drive screen addiction. Despite promising to help students focus on their feelings and affect and learn self-regulation, many of these digital products alienate students, commodify subjectivity, and undermine meaningful forms of learning. As schools adopt digital resilience programs, they become complicit in the conditions of meaninglessness and banalization that produce screen addiction and attention deficit and, in fact, significantly expand screen time in schools while furthering the economic interests of education profiteers. I conclude by suggesting that the antidote to the crisis of screen addiction should involve less of a focus on disciplinary control over youth access to screens and less digital resilience pedagogy and more of a focus on cultivating meaningful, critical, socially transformative, forms of education and social life through critical pedagogical practice.

Addictive Stimulation and Disenchantment: A Theory of Screen Addiction

There is a growing body of empirical research contending that screen exposure both makes children addicted to screens *and also* causes ADHD.[12] In this literature, screens are like drugs, and drugs, particularly stimulant drugs, are at the same time proposed as the remedy to ADHD caused by screens. Taken together the scholarship emphasizes the material and biological effects of screens, drugs, and the interplay between them. Some of this literature, such as in the prior endnote, emphasizes the correlation between screen usage in children and the development of ADHD symptoms. Other literature suggests that ADHD is a risk factor for screen addiction.[13] Yet other studies show a two-way correlation between ADHD and screen addiction.[14] Still other empirical literature locates the effects on the brain of heavy screen usage by children.[15] And other literature demonstrates that stimulant drugs such as methylphenidate (Adderall) temper "attention deficit" or distraction by imposing attentiveness and focus.[16] On the surface, these studies raise questions about ADHD and addictive screen usage as cause or effect of the other. Various studies in the above endnotes presume causality in one direction or the other. Some studies attempt to show ADHD as risk factor for screen addiction, and others show screen usage as risk factor for ADHD.

Taken together, however, these seemingly contradictory studies confirm a relationship between screen stimulation and drug stimulation that appears to be compensatory. That is, the stimulation of screens, when withdrawn, renders the experience of unmediated reality as unstimulating. Stimulant drugs can reinvest experience with the stimulation of screens when that stimulation has been withdrawn. Stimulant drugs such as amphetamine, nicotine, and caffeine, among others, allow users to pay attention to and focus on an object of learning or a task. Screen experience simultaneously stimulates physiologically and induces passivity of thought and receptivity to what is on the screen. For example, video provides the stimulating visual imagery that reading does not. Screens render non-screen experience (i.e., reality) banal, dull, and dim. What is more, the withdrawal of screen stimulation and the mode of passivity and reception leave the subject with a burden: the work of having to imagine, think, and interpret. To be clear, the medium itself does not inherently produce passivity and receptivity but rather the conventions of representation tend to do so, particularly in mass-produced corporate cultural production. These conventions of representation have to be learned by the viewer. There are countless examples of visual culture that open questions and foster radical imagination. There are also multiple traditions of critical scholarship (critical media literacy, critical pedagogy, cultural studies) that foster critical engagement with screen culture. These traditions teach students to interpret and analyze the meanings and ideologies produced by screen culture in relation to the formation of subjectivity and the political economy of the production, circulation, and consumption of visual culture.[17] However, such traditions of intellectual self-defense are seldom and rarely taught or institutionalized as part of formal schooling.

Both the empirical literature and the popular discourse on screen addiction and ADHD fail to consider what makes experience worth paying attention to. The public, educational, and medical discourses on ADHD bracket out the simple but crucial question of *why* students should pay attention to what it is that they are being told they ought to pay attention to. Framing the problem as an "attention deficit" quantifies the matter which is always qualitative while concealing the normative political and ethical values inherent in attention. That is, the framing of an "attention deficit" removes from attention the question of judgment and value, making attention a supposedly disinterested mechanism with an unquestionable value. In contrast, one of the earliest theorists of attention, William James, comprehended attention as ethical and intentional. Experience in James's view is what one agrees to attend to.[18] In fact, the crisis of youth screen addiction highlights the problem with the overdiagnosis of youth attention deficit. Screen addiction is most often considered as a kind of attention excess but for the allegedly wrong reasons—games, social media, videos, etc. The diagnosis of an "attention deficit" is typically discovered, rather, in the context of mandated forms of institutional control, often forms of education that are experienced by students as meaningless, decontextualized drudgery, as justified by authoritarian imposition or by an extrinsic promise of some future benefit such as academic advancement and monetary, career, and prosperity promises infinitely delayed. Screen addiction is threatening for precisely the same reasons. Instead of a lack of attention, the problem is attention to the wrong things. The crisis of screen addiction begs the question of what, for youth, is worth paying attention to?

Very often, that which is worth paying attention to is that which is meaningful, enchanting, or wondrous. Young children are enchanted by new experiences, wondrous objects, nature, experiment, and games of imagination. Robert Browning's poem "The Pied Piper of Hamlin" captures this enchantment of childhood in describing the lure of the piper whose playing promises "a joyous land where waters gushed and fruit trees grew, and everything put forth a fairer hue, and everything was *strange and new*." While in the poem the lure of the piper's music is a kind of seduction which draws children into a portal to be disappeared (taken by the Piper in lieu of the money owed him by the government and corporation), the description captures the enchantment of childhood itself, the time before the child is jaded by increased exposure to initially wondrous things. On the one hand, childhood provides novelty of experience, wonderment at the unforeseen. Yet, on the other hand, screens of all kinds add to reality a heightened experience: the stimulation of car crashes, bright lights, fast cuts, idealized versions of people and objects, horrific mutilations of bodies, stories of revenge, choreographed dance, inviting communities, sensual and sexual promises, encounters with monsters and angels, superheroes, recognition by strangers, affirmations from friends, and on and on.

Such stimulation functions on at least two levels. On one level, there is a sensual and visceral stimulation. On another level and wrapped up with the first is the way that digital sensual stimulation brings the viewer into ideological fantasies that are most often fantasies of power even as screen-use produces passivity, receptivity, and diffuses agency and action. The classic camera obscura definition of ideology is at work here, making reality appear inverted—in this case, passivity experienced as power. What are the ideological fantasies of power and agency wrapped up with the sensual stimulation of screens?: most often, the power to consume, the power to dominate others and nature, the power, as Freire observes, of the oppressor to desire freedom as the freedom to oppress others and make them unfree.

The point not to be missed is that screen addiction proffers a socially destructive and personally disempowering sense of agency. The passive stimulation of screens positions the subject as an object to be acted upon or to be inserted into a premade fantasy world of consumption. On the contrary, a critical conception of agency treats people as subjects, involves active engagement, interpretation, dialog, and interrogation of claims to truth, experiences, and others.

Ultimately, critical engagement creates the conditions for an active relation to experience and the capacity for action. Agency in the conception of critical pedagogy, for example, begins with meaningful experience, sees knowledge and interpretation as instruments for self and social understanding such that people can collectively intervene in public problems and challenge the social forces that produce oppressive experience. Agency in this view comprehends knowledge as a means of reflective action that liberates.

Following the use of screens, reality off-screens feels banal, boring, dim, and dull, and fails to grab our attention. We have grown accustomed to going to concerts, tourist attractions, parties, and sporting events where the crowd watches the live event through the screen of their phone. People are not only recording the live event in photos and videos, but they are also experiencing that reality as enhanced through the screen. Social media apps are designed to maximize their addictive powers and the inclination to check these apps, email, texts, and news feeds. Neurochemical rewards of checking reinforce the habit. As with other drugs, screen withdrawal results in cravings and, in some children and adults, tantrums.

Jonathan Crary points out that the sensuous experience of childhood and youth is replaced by addictive stimulation and homogeneity in what he terms the Internet Complex.[19] Youth, in Crary's view, are shut off from wonderment at the world they experience.[20] Wonderment involves contemplation, thinking, questioning, doubting, imagining, dreaming, and potentially dissenting or refusing. For this reason, Crary sees the decline in youth wonderment as tied to the decline in youth political rebellion.[21] The affirmation of experience renders the criticism of actually existing reality and the imagination of something better moot.

In Crary's view, wonderment at new experience is replaced by the "maelstrom of debilitating incoherence" and the "mass production of ignorance, stupidity, and hatefulness."[22] For Crary, as well as for Franco Berardi, the Internet Complex produces anomie and alienation, destroying social solidarity, and unending social relations necessary for individuals to make sense of the world and act on the world politically with others. Crary argues that what allows an intersubjective lifeworld is the stuff of flesh—voice, face, and gaze. The disembodiment accomplished by the Internet Complex estranges individuals from each other, from objects, and the natural world. Crary contends that we have lost our bodily connection to the world and consequently lost a holistic understanding of our relation to the world and the interconnectedness of all things.[23] For these contemporary critics and many others, the alienation of the internet is not only an instrument for undermining understanding and agency. It is sickening as well. Berardi locates the upturn of youth addiction, depression, and suicide with the destruction of community and solidarity, the isolation and feelings of powerlessness accomplished by internet culture.[24]

Not only the stimulation of screens and the rendering banal of reality promulgate stupidity and ignorance, and not only does the squirt of serotonin drive screen addiction. Also, these physiological responses testify to the lure of stimulated passivity, the abdication of action and agency, dropping the work of engagement with reality in favor of a mode of receptivity. The lure of stimulated passivity ought to be comprehended as akin to the psychological process whereby individuals, as Slavoj Zizek points out,[25] knowingly disavow that which they very well know oppresses them but they participate in it nonetheless. This is a process recognized by Horkheimer and Adorno at the end of "The Culture Industry" chapter of *Dialectic of Enlightenment*: "The triumph of advertising in the culture industry is that consumers feel compelled to buy and use its products even though they see through them" (167). The abdication of action and agency in favor of stimulated passivity becomes increasingly appealing as the "maelstrom of debilitating incoherence" of the internet produces an experience of social dislocation and a feeling of the incapacity to comprehend the social world in order to act with agency, to shape or inform the world one inhabits.

The problem of epistemic incoherence and stimulated passivity identified by Crary is deeply connected to the experience of social precarity fostered by unprecedented levels of economic inequality, the erosion of the capacity of local political action in the face of global corporate power (as Zygmunt Bauman observed)[26] as well as the rise of authoritarian political movements that aim to provide the false security of the strongman amidst growing material and symbolic precarity.[27] Such authoritarian movements and leaders actively seek to erode the knowledge-based means to comprehend and act on the social world, spreading lies and undermining the institutions of knowledge including schools and media.

The disenchantment produced by the passive stimulation of screens expresses the deeper logic of technological modernity, Enlightenment science, and the project of disenchantment of the lifeworld through rationalization. As Crary points out, this inanimates and disconnects the holistic relations between living things, undermining not only social relations but, as well, relations of the self to the natural world. Fostered by the Internet Complex, estrangement abets the extractive razing of the earth in pursuit of profit. Such alienation from the living world makes the representational world of screens appear as the only world one can know.

In the realm of digital disenchantment, reality is experienced as alienated, abstract, and lacking economic justice and institutions of care, and the desire for wealth trumps all. As I write this, I regularly listen to Chicago Public School teachers recount how their students now mostly dream of getting rich by becoming internet influencers, celebrities, or sports stars. These students believe that they can become rich through representing the use of consumer goods to others, and they do not dream of pursuing vocations that benefit the public or planet, that care for others. Agency in these accounts is strictly personal and expressed through internet fantasy of entrepreneurialism and consumerism. Of course, such consumer conceptions of agency not only undermine better social and political conceptions of agency (such as democratic and critical ones), but they also participate in disappearing the social implications of one's actions from the material implications of them. In this troubled view, problems can only be framed as personal problems. What is necessary are pedagogies that foster in students the capacities and inclinations to translate their personal problems into public problems and to theorize collective acts of public intervention. Such pedagogies need to be seen as necessary not only in schools but throughout public culture.

Franco Berardi writes that in semio-capitalism, alienation is exploding, while economic behavior and mental pathology are interdependent. The epidemic of mass shootings (with schools as a major site of such shootings) belies the crisis of agency. As Berardi argues in *Heroes*, the frenzied attempt to recover agency through explosive violence provides a final act of control—control over life and death as remedy to a life devoid of agency and a future experienced as beyond any control.[28] The shooters are nearly all white, heterosexual, and male, yet the rash of teenage female suicides, driven to a great extent by social media, seems to follow the same logic.[29] For Berardi, the pathologies of semio-capitalism derive from the subjective experience of finite cyber time being at odds with the infinite natures of cyber space. To be inundated with an endless flow of information but to have a limited human capacity to process or mediate it results in an acceleration of informational stimulation but a shrinking of the collective psyche and collective skin.[30]

The corporeal and psychic effects of virtualization merge a discourse of cyber utopianism with neoliberal ideology.[31] Cyber utopianism frames the internet and new technology as promising ever greater progress, freedom, information, efficiency, and fun while neoliberalism suggests that specifically market-related uses of such technology enable these promises. This merging of cyber utopianism and neoliberalism confers a conception of agency defined by participation in online consumption, 24/7 work/leisure connectivity with no end or outside, and the obligatory constant fabrication of a cyber avatar of one's subjectivity consuming things and experiences. Screen addiction and the crisis of agency are thoroughly wrapped up with these ideologies that make people feel that their subjectivity is in constant threat of evaporating if they are not seen by others online, responding to others online, or cultivating fantasy worlds of consumption through online activity. Zygmunt Bauman describes this "subjectivity fetishism" in *Consuming Life*:

> In the society of consumers no one can become a subject without first turning into a commodity, and no one can keep his or her subjectness secure without perpetually resuscitating, resurrecting and replenishing the capacities expected and required of a sellable commodity. The "subjectivity" of the "subject", and most of what that subjectivity enables the subject to achieve, is focused on an unending effort to itself become, and remain, a sellable commodity.[32]

Bauman's insight highlights that screen addiction is not only driven by neurobiological stimulation and behaviorist rewards built into social media apps. It is also imbricated with the structuring of particular forms of embodied ideological selfhood within a particular social context—in this case not just consumer capitalism but semiocapitalism in which commerce in data and production of data about the self are central to the economy (think Tinder, or even LinkedIn). Neoliberal cyber utopianism amplifies subjectivity fetishism through social media sites rendering real people into commodified data. Such subjectivity fetishism does not facilitate an understanding of the forces and structures that inform and produce the subject nor does it catalyze understanding of how subjects can remake the social world through reflective action. Screen addiction needs to be comprehended as an inherent feature of semio-capitalism that falsely positions digital technology as a force that is beyond human agency and control while also conferring a pedagogy of consumer subjectivity. This is a subjectivity that is at once passive and spectatorial, alienated and commodified and yet demands of each individual constant work to fabricate a representation of the self to others. In the context of youth and schooling, the imperatives for students to produce digital representations of self needs to be comprehended as part of a growing capture of uncompensated child labor in the making of children into data production engines via digital education products.

Producing Passive Stimulation on Screens in School with the False Promises of Digital Resilience Products

Digital disenchantment, alienation, commodified subjectivity, and the crisis of agency that drive screen addiction are particularly evident in the slew of recently developed digital products that have become commonplace in schools. Digital SEL resilience programs that, under a guise of getting students in touch with their emotions, promise to unblock emotional, affective, and behavioral impediments to learning such that students can become good empty receptacles for the depositing of knowledge. These digital screen products promise to teach students self-regulation and instill discipline. However, they vastly expand school screen time and school commercialism while intensifying alienation and undermining agency.

A glaring example of these efforts is the school social media app Class Dojo that is now in the vast majority of US classrooms. It is a form of digital surveillance that was able to get into schools by being offered without charge.[33] In addition to providing teachers with a tool to send parents photos and videos of their children along with text and emoticons, it purports to teach students "mindfulness" techniques of individual self-control with animated videos. Videos feature animated characters such as Mojo, who looks like a green condom with a Karate-style headband, and an odd prevalence of cycloptic cartoon characters who instruct students about mindfulness, optimism, moods, and respect. The in-class program includes a behaviorist system of awarding students points for their affect. As a system of classroom surveillance, it approximates what Foucault described as a normalizing judge that examines to normalize: comparing, differentiating, and hierarchically ranking.[34] Such mindfulness supposedly counters students' distraction and disinterest.

The company profits by taking student data and using it to market services in SEL and mindfulness to parents as pay for fee services. As I have discussed in my book *The Disaster of Resilience,* these programs in SEL do not teach students how to understand their feelings and emotions by helping them comprehend the social causes of what they are experiencing. Instead, they employ animated cartoons to encourage students to notice emotions but then employ techniques like breathing exercises and visualization to "lock feelings away" so that students can supposedly be unblocked receptacles of knowledge and information. Class Dojo exemplifies a bevy of screen products that promise to unblock impediments to learning that are framed as caused by student distraction. These digital products in SEL largely embrace a disciplinary view of student learning and transmission models of pedagogy that presume that knowledge can be standardized, homogenized, and ever more efficiently delivered and deposited in students.

Both the standards and accountability movement in education (teaching to the test, standardizing and homogenizing supposedly objective and neutral curriculum, disregarding student experience and culture) and the purported remedy to it in the form of subjectivist resilience and SEL programs and products disregard student experience, meaning, and culture. For example, Centervention's ZooU program in SEL uses onscreen animated avatars in social settings to model "appropriate" social interaction on screens in classrooms. This product purports to foster social and emotional skills by taking students out of social interaction with other human beings and putting students in front of screens to play video games. Amira Learning's scripted digital reading program replaces human reading instruction between teachers and students with a student in front of a screen. None of these products is capable of relating learning to the social context, culture, or experience of the student the way a teacher can through dialog with students. These products alienate students from teachers, from other students, and from the process of learning while alienating knowledge from the self and the social world.

Class Dojo positions teachers as needing to cultivate online imagery of their capacity. Its mindfulness material promises that it will help students "tame the beast" of what they are feeling. This program's mindfulness content does not help students understand why they are feeling what they are feeling or understand what forces, structures, and interests are behind feelings of sadness, anxiety, or anger. Students subject to the program in urban school districts with rates of poverty approaching 100 percent do not learn what produces the poverty, inequality, community violence, symbolic violence of racism, radical upward material distribution, prisonized and militarized schools and communities, nor the depression, despair, hopelessness, fear, and insecurity that accompany such material and symbolic social conditions. Instead, this animated program encourages students to, for example, imagine putting their bad feelings in a box attached to a helium balloon and watching the bad feelings float away into the sky. Or it encourages them to do breathing exercises. These examples illustrate how screen addiction is pedagogically produced by these educational products that foster passive stimulation, alienation, and commodified subjectivity. Similarly, Go Noodle—a widely adopted app with mindfulness exercises, guides students to breath and overcome "feeling frozen—a feeling we all experience." This app shows students an animated child made of ice and has them imagine melting into a puddle. Students are told to tighten and relax their muscles until they are fully melted. Again, the assumption is that if students can be attentive to their breath and bodies, they can modify the vague bad feelings that they have, and this promises that they will be "ready to learn."

Whether students are frozen with rage, fear, or another emotion is not clear from the product. Neither identifying the feelings that they have nor discussing what it is that they have experienced that produces such feelings is a part of this instruction. However, the melting exercise could not be clearer in its aim of making a docile and compliant body. As well, this exercise could not be clearer that the body and its feelings are obstacles to the mental work of schooling framed as knowledge consumption rather than meaningful dialogic exchange. These kinds of mindfulness SEL apps illustrate human capital discourse and its advocacy of developing students' non-cognitive skills for docility and self-control to get the body and its feelings out of the way so that transmission models of pedagogy can successfully dump knowledge into children. Not only do such programs fail to make students' feelings and bodies into objects of critical analysis for students to comprehend how what they are experiencing subjectively relates to what they are being asked to learn about; also, such programs fail to relate knowledge to lived experience and the social world that students inhabit that produces the feelings that they have. Digital resilience products such as these alienate students from their feelings and experiences by misdirecting them about how to interpret and understand the social origins of their feelings. They frame emotion and experience as burden and blockage rather than as objects of critical analysis to be theorized and interpreted to identify and intervene against the public problems that produce emotion and experience.

These screen products in schools mystify the social origins of what is subjectively experienced, asking students to focus on new-agey techniques of corporeal self-control: breathing exercises, visualization. Yet other for-profit digital SEL products are marketed as teaching character with games and avatars such as Character Strong or Centervention's "Adventures Aboard the S.S. Grin." These programs largely teach virtues such as courage, respect, and kindness as individual traits that apply in interpersonal situations and are a matter of individual responsibility rather than framing virtuous action as a consequence of ethical social contexts that foster, cultivate, and reward virtuous action.

In this way such programs actively produce ignorance about the relationships between knowledge, subjectivity, and objectivity. Furthermore, these kinds of mindfulness programs aim to capture student attention, producing passive stimulation through animation, music, and narration and to disinvite them from feelings of fear, anger, and sadness. These programs very well could highlight holistically the ways emotions come from more than the self and the body but also from material circumstances (hunger, homelessness, and violence are experienced at high rates in urban districts), social relations of domination and subordination, and symbolic violence, including positioning the very working-class, poor, Black, and brown students such programs target as inherently criminal, deficient, oppositional, out of control, and lazy. Were SEL programs to take seriously the social and emotions, they would address how the experience of the self is wrapped up with relations of power.

They would also highlight how the process of learning is imbricated with social, political, and educational antagonisms that are lived out in the school but informed by larger structures and social tendencies in the world including class antagonism, structures of white supremacy, and patriarchy that organize the social world and institutions hierarchically. They would comprehend, as well, that a social understanding of the self in which the self is both a social product and a force for making a different kind of society. In such a pedagogy, the affirmational character of mindfulness curriculum would give way to critical forms of curriculum that comprehend oppressive feelings as coming from oppressive social forces that make oppressive contexts. Here, the process of comprehending the self and society creates the conditions for collective action and agency to aspire to transform the causes that produce what is experienced.

From Screen Addiction to Critical Pedagogy: Enchantment, Meaning, and Agency

In *Dialectic of Enlightenment*, Horkheimer and Adorno address how the logic of enlightenment rationality (reason through bureaucratization, calculation, and exchange) aims to overcome mythology and irrationalism. Enlightenment rationality aims to disenchant the world by making all experience into numbers and utility, by eradicating difference and indeterminacy, and by appropriating that which is different into repetitions of the same. The Enlightenment rationality logic of unity, totality, harmony, quantification, and eradication of difference results in not only the overcoming of myth but a movement toward a frenzy of rationalization. This movement creates new barbarisms as, contradictorily, we celebrate its progress defined through industry, capitalist accumulation, positivism, and technologization. Horkheimer and Adorno were writing in the 1940s and witnessed their nation—seen as the pinnacle of Enlightenment progress in philosophy, technology, arts, and commerce—develop into a murderous mythically driven rationalized regime. Perhaps the biggest and most destructive ongoing expression of the dialectic of Enlightenment is the myth that capitalist economic growth can continue indefinitely even as capitalist progress has resulted in dire environmental crisis, increased economic polarization, and political turmoil.

Rational progress and technological development aim for maximizing profit at the expense of both humans and the nature they depend on. Today's applications of the heights of digital and pharmacological technology on children repeat the dialectic of Enlightenment and the path of this form of rationality toward irrationalism. We see this in the drugging of students into attention for the purposes of gaming test score outcomes that are erroneously described as "learning." We also see this in the making of students into data production engines by putting them on dubious educational technology products. The fetish for increasing the numbers and churning out data obscures the meaning and purpose of learning and the social uses and import of learning for self and collective social benefit. The metrics fetish presumes an impossible endless inclusion into exclusionary capitalist labor markets. We see this in programs that claim to be teaching students to understand their emotions and develop self-regulation by replacing human interaction and dialog with screen time and AI avatars in schools such that student affect can be measured, quantified, and rendered as data. For example, the digital SEL products and online curriculum are quantifying and datafying student behavior, demanding that teachers track students in real time with data management dashboards and app-based check in tools. These programs put students to work doing uncompensated labor making commercially valuable data for technology companies.

Such instrumental rationality leading to irrationalism is at work in the faith in digital programs and products. The translation of knowledge and affect into quantified data falsely appears as a promise of ever greater control and ever-increasing efficiencies of learning systems. Yet, these programs and products repeat the positivism of standardized testing, delinking the values, assumptions, ideologies, and meanings from the claims to truth falsely positioned as neutral, disinterested, and objective. The SEL apps that are selling contracts in digital products in schools are not facilitating the comprehension of how private and personal feelings and experiences are produced by broader social, systemic, and structural forces and antagonisms. These products disallow the translation of privately experienced problems into the public problems animating them.[35] Instead, under the rubric of technological progress, quantifiability, and control these products defeat understanding of the relationships between claims to truth and the social, political, historical contexts and contests that make them meaningful. Such digital products promote ways of seeing that are affirmative of the visible realities without allowing students to negate, reject, or demystify the objects of experience by socially situating them. In the face of these technologies, the critical move is to situate feeling in relation to comprehending, confronting, and opposing the growing urgent and intertwined crises of militarism, war, fascism, environmental devastation, capitalism, and scapegoating of difference.

Crary highlights the connection between the creativity of reverie, imagination, and engagement with perplexing images. He worries that digital technology routinizes vision, shutting down the capacity of the subject to experience reality in complex ways rather than through singular vision tied to commerce and instrumentalism.[36] One of the things that can allow individuals to experience the world in complex ways is theory. Critical pedagogy makes theory an indispensable instrument for interpreting experience. Theory facilitates the investigation of values, assumptions, and ideologies that undergird practices and claims to truth. Theory also allows for contextualizing and interpreting assertions in relation to broader systemic and structural forces and social tendencies. Theory allows people to think about what they do and to comprehend experiences in terms of ethics, politics, and history. Theory is a tool for agency and a means of breaking out of the thought stifling strictures of positivism and its reduction of the world to decontextualized number and fact. Theory allows people to locate themselves in terms of broader material and symbolic contests, connect their practices to their vision for the future, and cultivate the radical imagination.

Educators can collaborate with students to break out of the passive stimulation of screens and reject screen addiction as a constructed crisis that cynically frames individuals as little more than objects overwhelmed by technological forces. Educators can cultivate critical forms of agency by teaching students how to theorize their experience (including learning to critically theorize screen experience) and the social context they inhabit. They can foster students' critical dispositions that enable them to relate claims to truth to the social authority, positions, interests, and ideological assumptions of knowledge producers. The promise in learning to theorize, understand, and develop projects for change with others stands to transform the site of school from one of obedience, alienation, and drudgery to one of meaning, interest, and social power.

3

Raging Hormones: Transgender Youth and the Ideology of Competition

The political right has organized a campaign of hate directed at transgender youth and transgender people more broadly. Right-wing activists and legislators in the United States have passed hundreds of laws censoring books about transgender people and non-heteronormative forms of sexuality and placed restrictions on teachers to speak or teach about gender and sexuality.[1] At the Conservative Political Action Conference (CPAC) in 2023 and 2024, Michael Knowles, a keynote speaker, called for "eradicating transgender identity."[2] The US trend is aligned with a global movement toward fascist politics in multiple countries that aims to stitch together racist nationalism with a revival of patriarchy and religious fundamentalism.[3] This rightist campaign has two principle aspects centered on education. One attack is focused on transgender athletes, alleging unfair athletic competition by male to female trans youth. The other element of the hate campaign involves censoring teachers, curriculum, and books and keeping bathrooms gender segregated. The spectacle of unfair school athletic competition frames testosterone as an unfair competitive advantage. The censoring of books and curriculum and prohibiting teachers from teaching about sexuality are alleged by proponents to be protecting children and families by defending the heteronormative nuclear family.

The right's attack on trans and gay rights and identity is a major part of a right-wing populist political project to stitch together a broader tripartite ideology. The Republican Party in the United States has borrowed from Victor Orban in Hungary and Georgia Meloni in Italy whose fascist political movements claim to value the three F's: Faith, Family, and Freedom. The fascist movement makes transphobic and homophobic sentiment central as it attempts to construct national community through nostalgia for a lost or threatened valuation of the sacred family as the fundamental unit of hyper-nationalism.[4] The sacred family in this assertion is a heterosexual one claimed to be the natural order ordained by God and particularly by fundamentalist Christianity. Should there be any doubts about how far into the mainstream of Republican politics this fundamentalist Christianity reaches, at the 2024 CPAC a speaker, Jack Prosobiec (cheered on onstage by Steve Bannon the leading strategist of the MAGA movement), held up a cross and announced his intention to "overthrow democracy" and replace it with Christianity.[5]

This articulation of reactionary politics carries on a long-standing neoliberal tendency to make the family the fundamental social unity, repeating Thatcher's famous statement that there is no such thing as society, only individuals and families. The point of such a denial of society and elevation of the family is to defund public goods and services and shift the onus for social supports from society to the patriarchal family.

As well, the right links these notions of family and religion to the promise of economic nationalism as an alternative to neoliberal globalization (framed by the right as "globalism"—an anti-semitically coded term intimating a global Jewish conspiracy). As Nancy Fraser points out, Trumpism represented a grand bait-and-switch in which he ran on economic nationalism (trade wars, anti-immigration) yet pursued neoliberal economic policies (tax cuts on the rich, efforts to privatize and defund public goods and services, appointment of billionaires to secretaryships).[6] "Freedom" in this context means freedom from collective responsibility for the material support of and recognition of others, even as "freedom" functions as a call to jingoistic patriotism toward a native-born national community that is exclusionary and circumscribed through Whiteness, Christianity, patriarchy, and heteronormativity. Indeed, if there is another group as aggressively maligned by the authoritarian populist right, it is immigrants. Like trans and gay people, their vilification serves as a constitutive outside for the forging of this new fascist politics.

Within the right's political imaginary, women and men have different traditional familial, labor, and social roles. Women are natural caregivers and nurturers. Men are natural leaders and protectors. More women ought to be encouraged to be stay-at-home mothers (this represents a nostalgia for a male single-earner family that, in its post–Second World War heyday, was hardly universal in the United States —it was always racially restricted and was to a great extent the consequence of labor unions). Girls and boys in this view ought to dress in clothing that is "masculine" or "feminine" and that corresponds to gender assigned at birth. The war on transgender identity is thus an effort to reassert not only a fragile and failing family unit but also to claim the naturalness of the gendered division of labor, including the unpaid "second shift" and the exploited feminized vocations. As Robin Truth Goodman elaborates, "[G]ender 'realness' can be seen as the body's literalization of the division of labor or the society of exchange *against diversity*."[7] While this is evident in the underpaying of feminized caregiving labor, it is also clear in the pattern of gendered division of academic labor from early childhood education to higher education.

The authoritarian right positions trans identity as a threat to its vision of a patriarchal, Christo-fascist, hyper-nationalist order. The right grounds gender through nature by reference to religion and biology: both god's "natural order" and the assertion that gender can be grounded in biological reproductive capacity. Trans in this discourse represents a challenge to the alleged nature of gender as it demonstrates gender as constructed rather than natural, unmoored from biological determination and reproductive function and delinked from some prescribed patriarchal order. The right's vilification of trans includes ascription to trans people of "unnatural" choice, and it positions trans adults generally and trans teachers specifically as a threat to children. The right alleges trans adults "groom" and "recruit" children, dangerously giving them the idea that they too do not have to live in the gender assigned to them at birth but might choose a different gender.

In response to the question of why the right has put its crosshairs on trans people, a number of liberal critics have suggested that this is a matter of scapegoating trans people by an authoritarian movement.[8] Scapegoating trans people displaces blame for economic issues such as poverty, inequality, and political issues such as the steady erosion of democratic governance and concentrated rule, particularly by economic elites. This brand of hatemongering finds purchase with a far-right electoral base.

While the liberal scapegoating explanation is true, this explanation does not address why it is that the trans community in particular has an enormous cultural-symbolic significance to the right's political imaginary and a crucial political economic aspect. Namely, what the right's anxiety about gender and sexuality belies is a steady erosion of dimorphic gender categories. Transgender, non-binary, and non-heterosexual identities have become mainstream through mass media, social media, the mainstreaming of constructivist social theory, and changes to law. Traditional dimorphic gender difference has increasingly come into question as well through pharmacological and medical manipulations of the body.[9] The right's anxiety about the breakdown of the patriarchal heteronormative family represents a concern over loss of control over the biological, cultural, and economic reproduction of society on its terms—white heteronormative capitalism.[10]

The liberal defense of the trans community is largely grounded in values of multicultural difference. In multicultural discourse, trans identity is one of many non-dominant gender and sexual identities that deserve cultural and political recognition. In this view, non-dominant identities deserve inclusion into predominantly heteronormative institutions such as family (and the legal benefits that support it) and schooling, as well as political culture and the private sector. As Nancy Fraser has termed it, this "progressive neoliberal" perspective (sometimes referred to as "corporate multiculturalism") calls for cultural recognition and inclusion into a neoliberal political economic order without consideration for the ways that cultural difference is imbricated with class inequality and exclusion.[11] In the "progressive" neoliberal framing, we can all compete for scarce resources and more different cultural groups can be included into this competition yet valuation of difference should not be comprehended in terms of redistributive justice, that is, the democratization of control over capital and the redistribution of wealth to effect economic equality with particular attention to how class inequality is lived through cultural differences.

When it comes to educational issues, the implications of these different views on trans identity are distinct. The right is legislating against the expression of trans identity in school, trans school athletes competing in school sports, gender neutral bathrooms, and teachers teaching about trans and other gender and sexual identities. In a word: exclusion. Liberals are advocating the inclusion of trans athletes in school sports as well as teaching about trans and other "minority" gender and sexual identities.

The right contends that curriculum and library books about gay, trans, and other non-heteronormative identities ought to be censored or banned. Similarly, teachers ought to be prevented from teaching about sexuality. The right justifies these efforts at censorship largely on the grounds of conservative Christian morality, by framing children as innocent and devoid of sexuality, and framing non-heteronormative non-patriarchal forms of gender and sexuality as perverse, deviant, unnatural, and contagious. The right conflates non-heteronormative forms of gender and sexuality with pedophilia to claim that trans and gay people are "grooming" children. Claims of "grooming" children simultaneously muddle allegations of influencing sexual knowledge, sexual orientation, and gender orientation with allegations of sexual predation on children—as if same-sex desire is the same as desire for children and as if the desire for gender reassignment is the same as desire for children. The right also asserts that the problem with trans students playing school sports is that it is unfair competition when a formerly male student competes against female students. These arguments commonly allege testosterone is an unfair natural advantage in the bodies of MtF athletes. Liberals respond by asserting the primacy of values of recognition of youth gender and sexual difference and of inclusion into existing institutions and the social order. They also emphasize these values over concerns with competitive fair play, pointing to empirical evidence in competitive sports outcomes that suggest no biological advantage.

From the traditions of critical theory, another set of views of trans politics upends both the rightist and liberal positions. Inspired by Michel Foucault's *History of Sexuality*, Judith Butler and Paul B. Preciado advance constructivist conceptions of gender and sexuality.[12] In these views gender and sexuality are primarily discursive. That is, there is nothing essential about gender and sexual identity categories. Neither nature nor biology grounds claims about gender and sexuality. Rather, they are profoundly historical, social, and cultural fictions, narratives, sets of ideas, and collections of material practices. Foucault provides a way of comprehending how discourse creates subject positions that organize behaviors and practices. Knowledge-making activities in institutions produce identity categories. The discursive creation of the categories enabled behavior to be translated into states of being, categories of personhood in ways that had been priorly unintelligible. Similarly, the "nature" of gender difference has changed radically in the past few hundred years. The constructivist perspective does not deny the materiality of different bodies but rather shows how material differences are organized through meaning-making, knowledge producing activities in institutions. For example, schools produce gender difference through countless practices such as gender-differentiated sports teams, gendered extracurricular activities, gendered assumptions about play, curriculum, gender-informing teachers pedagogical practices and expectations of different students, and, of course, the gender-segregated bathroom.

Judith Butler's performative theory shares with Foucault's a recognition that subjects are "spoken by" discourse and, in turn, bodies speak and perform discourse. Her early work highlighted that sex is a fiction added to the fiction of gender rather than gender being a function of sexual reproductive difference.[13] She emphasizes that *all* gender is performed, that being "a man" or being "a woman" are "internally unstable affairs,"[14] and that resistance to hegemonic norms of gender can happen through the repetition with a difference of dominant discourse of gender and sexuality. Writing about Jennie Livingston's documentary film *Paris Is Burning* about drag balls of gay and trans men and women in New York City in the late 1980s, Butler is worth quoting at length:

> To claim that all gender is like drag, or is drag, is to suggest that "imitation" is at the heart of the *heterosexual* project and its gender binarisms, that drag is not a secondary imitation that presupposes a prior and original gender, but that hegemonic heterosexuality is itself a constant and repeated effort to imitate its own idealizations. That it must repeat this imitation, that it sets up pathologizing practices and normalizing sciences in order to produce and consecrate its own claim on originality and propriety, suggests that heterosexual performativity is beset by an anxiety that it can never

fully overcome, that is, effort to become its own idealizations can never be finally or fully achieved, and that it is consistently haunted by that domain of sexual possibility that must be excluded for heterosexualized gender to produce itself. In this sense, then, drag is subversive to the extent that it reflects on the imitative structure by which hegemonic gender is itself produced and disputes heterosexuality's claim on naturalness and originality.[15]

Butler's comprehension of gender and sexuality as discursive, performative, and always imitative runs contrary to the essentialism and claims to naturalness of gender in the right-wing views. As well, the constructivist view challenges the liberal multicultural perspective that maintains the centrality, dominance, and naturalness of heteronormative gender ideology even as it allows for toleration and inclusion of gender and sexual "minority" positions. The constructivist view highlights the extent to which dominant and, indeed, all gender and sexuality depend upon the discursive formation of subject positions and identity categories for people to occupy. To put it differently, for gender and sexuality to determine where people are placed within the social order, people must be ongoingly educated into the dominant heteronormative gender ideologies/fictions as though they were natural reality.

Following from Foucault as well as selectively appropriating from Althusser's theory of subject formation, "interpellation,"[16] Butler's conception of subjectivity does not provide a systematic account for how gender performativity is imbricated with political economy and the reproduction of class hierarchy and inequality. Paul B. Preciado builds on both Foucault and Butler by accounting for how the discursive construction of gender is forged not just through the signifying practices of discourse but also through the manipulation of bodies, particularly through pharmaceutical and digital communication technologies and legacies of racialized colonialism. Preciado provides an account for how the history of gender is wrapped up with the history of the development of technologies of body control such as gender reassignment surgery, the pill, the use of hormones to regulate reproduction, stimulate or constrict sexual desire. Manipulation through body routines, though, does not end with such medical interventions but include everyday practices like eating, exercising, dressing, buying, reading, and interacting: it is not a trend that belongs only to a minority population but rather a much more ubiquitous connection to capital circulation and consumerism.

Yet, in Preciado's view, the discursive construction of gender and sexual identity is imbricated most fundamentally with the power of global pharmaceutical and media corporations that aim to channel "orgasmic force" (what Deleuze and Guattari refer to as "desiring-production"[17]) into traditional gendered forms of subjectivity conducive to corporate capital accumulation. What is at stake in this for Preciado is the ways these heteronormative gendering practices and institutions dominate, exploit, and hierarchically organize people while (1) restricting the potential for the pursuit of pleasures, creativities, and a multiplicity of forms of life, and (2) restricting the capacity of people to collectively control the conditions of their lives. Paul B. Preciado employs an auto theoretical method of experimentation with his own body, self-administering testosterone and recounting the mutations and malleability of the body. Preciado denaturalizes male, female, heterosexual, homosexual, and trans identity by showing how the material and symbolic making of subject positions defies our capacity to tease out what, for example, hormones physically do as distinct from what hormones mean. Preciado demonstrates how the regime of traditional gender depends upon corporate chemical and communicational manipulation of the body completely divorced from nature. Preciado's experiments aim to take the chemical and communicational manipulation of the body in a different direction—one of gender and sexual multiplicity, malleability, mutability, and agency over established categorizations.

Preciado points to the ways that people are on a large scale formed as gender and sexual subjects through the imposition of hormonal and digital technological manipulations. On an individual level Preciado imagines everyone being able to experiment on themselves, to be liberated of constraining categories of gender and sexuality. On a collective level, Preciado imagines common projects in which people together seize control of the means of producing bio-codes. This involves the possibility of collectively seizing control of the production, distribution, and use of material such as drugs and hormones as well as the pedagogies and symbolic cultural infrastructure that makes gender and sex and channels them into exploitative relations. This vision of what Preciado calls "bio-communism" extends to the economy more broadly as he sees all capitalist activity being undergirded by desiring-production. By exploding categories of gender and sexuality, Preciado aims to take apart both the gendered division of labor and the ways that capitalist accumulation works in our "pharmacopornographic" era. Preciado's perspective highlights the interconnections of cultural politics and political economy. The deconstruction of gender and sexuality for Preciado is connected to a broader project of living in common in which collective control over collective labor results in shared benefit.

Central to Preciado's thought is a recognition that people get educated into oppressive and dominant hegemonic forms of gender and sexuality. There is a distinctly pedagogical dimension to Preciado's project. Preciado devised educational workshops for re-educating people to recognize the construction of gender and sexuality and to develop agency and transformative projects. Preciado emphasizes that the goal is not greater inclusion into existing categories and oppressive, confining practices of gender and sexuality. Preciado wants everyone to engage in radical experimentation with their body and sense of self. Self in this view is comprehended by disidentification rather than identity as self-sameness or identity as identification with preformed (symbolic) identity categories.

Here the distinction from the liberal multicultural view is particularly stark. For liberal multiculturalists "discovering one's identity" is a matter of identifying with already existing pre-constituted identity categories. Preciado emphasizes that self-hood is process and experiment and has at its core a kind of non-recognition or misrecognition. Nobody fully fits pre-constituted identity categories. To illustrate Preciado's point, take for example, Josh Hawley, the US Congressman who has been one of the most outspoken far-right advocates calling for the "eradication of trans identity." Hawley came to national attention for his masculine pose of putting his fist in the air to salute January 6, 2021 insurrectionists. Hawley, who is married with children, has been subject to vast speculation on the internet that he himself is not fully the straight man he plays in political spectacle and demands of others as the only acceptable gender and sexual identity position for all.[18] Social media circulates pictures and comments of Hawley kissing his wife with a look of revulsion, picks apart his personal appearance alleging femininity, suggests that only someone not so secure in their gender and sexuality would make such an issue out of the desires and practices of others. Hawley is haunted online by the possibility that there may be more to his identity than his exhortations. For a politician whose identity is utterly wrapped up with the constant curation and cultivation with his own online self-presentation, would not the massive volume of speculation, questioning, and images at the very least introduce questions and doubts? He might ask himself: do I really look feminine? Why did I really have a dormitory poster of a male model in college? How do I reconcile my denunciations of pornography with my seditious support for a former president who committed crimes involving an affair with a porn star and sexual assault? Why do I appear to be grimacing in these photos of me kissing my wife? Is my wife really a woman? Is there a desire in me that my will might not be able to contain and that my body betrays as captured on camera?

Section II. How Schools Make Gendered Subjects of Production, Consumption, and Exclusion

The prior chapters detailed how pharmaceutical drugs and screen stimulation products are implicated in making youth subjectivity in forms conducive to capitalist accumulation. Students are induced to take stimulant drugs such as Adderall and Ritalin for focus and attention to manage affect and become more effective receptacles for the depositing of knowledge and information. As well, digital technology produces corporeal stimulation and excitation that challenge the institutional imperatives of schools to make docile and disciplined bodies—usually in ways that are conducive to social relations of production. Increasingly, schools are sites where students produce data for technology corporations.

Social and cultural reproduction during the industrial era of schooling aimed to teach skills and know-how for work but most crucially wrapped in ideologies intended to teach social relations of production. In the industrial era, working-class schools taught dispositions of submission to authority, quantification of progress, competition rather than collaboration. Professional-class schools taught skills and know-how for higher education with dispositions for managing the private and public sectors. Such dispositions included dialog and debate. Students largely learned time- and labor-intensive forms of learned self-control.

During the neoliberal postindustrial economy, social and cultural reproduction changed. The management and control of the body took on increasingly direct forms such as repressive pedagogies, the administration of drugs to manage attention, focus, and emotion. Preciado terms the current era the "pharmacopornographic" era which shares elements with the postindustrial neoliberal era but has certain key differences. According to Preciado the economy has been overtaken by the production and trade in sensual stimulation via pharmaceuticals and digital technology. Preciado explains the objective of pharmacopornographic technology is the material and discursive production of the body through stimulation for capital's reproduction of the species. Preciado points to the extractive trafficking in hormones and other drugs that transform human cells into capital.

A particularly clear educational case in point not mentioned by Preciado is the capturing of student attention in part through pharmaceutical stimulants for the educational industry in digital curriculum materials, online learning platforms and other digital products. The pharmaceuticals stimulate students' bodies for focus and attention in place of meaningful, contextually relevant, and critical forms of learning that would draw student attention due to the explanatory power they have for the self and the social world. The digital educational products stimulate students for attention capture toward the end as well of transmission models of pedagogy. And digital screen technologies stimulate students outside of school, drawing eyeballs to content that delivers advertising revenue and that impresses students into working uncompensated to produce commercially valuable data—data captured by hundreds of corporations with every touch of the screen.

Preciado refers to the "pornification of labor" in the post-Fordist economy. While Preciado is writing about the commodification of sex and the ways that mainstream culture industries are modeled on the pornography industry, he is explaining a much broader transformation of the entire economy and the self. Preciado writes that in order to comprehend the making of post-Fordist labor through the making of subjectivity, it is necessary to consider how capitalist production is informed by the consumption and production of (1) drugs: "all biologically active legal or illegal substances that are able to modify the metabolism of the cells on which they work" (274), texts and visual signs included; (2) audiovisual material: "audiovisual technique capable of modifying the sensibility and production of desire, of activating cycles of excitation-frustration and the production of psychosomatic pleasure, in fine of capturing the body's system of affect production" (275); and (3) "sexual labor" "The transformation of a body's 'potentia gaudendi' ['orgasmic force' or desiring-production] into a commodity by a contract (more or less formal) of service" (275). While Preciado focuses on the trade in sexuality at the core of the post-Fordist economy (the pornography industry, the centrality of sex to the selling of commodities, the production of libidinal desire in all economic activity), his model applies to the ways that economies in drugs, audiovisual material, and affective labor are now at the center of schooling. The industries in affective labor include the countless digital apps and programs that sell curriculum, the direct instruction AI reading avatar programs, the biometric surveillance and pedagogy products, the SEL, mindfulness, growth mindset, and mediation programs.

Preciado writes that "the power of these three platforms [drugs, AV, sex] for the production of capital rests in their ability to function as *prostheses* of subjectivity" (275). In the context of schooling, the convergence of drugs, screens, and their uses to capture affect serves the process of producing particular forms of subjectivity via the manipulation of both biocodes and the symbolic codes which forge consciousness and shape bodies and bodily practices. Preciado points out that the extractive trafficking in hormones and other drugs turns cells into capital.[19] In schools, the trafficking in attention and focus drugs but also in hormones such as the pill, widely prescribed to girls after puberty, makes the student's body into an engine for capital. The taking of the pill, as Preciado points out, produces gendered knowledge, gendered rituals, a gendered ordering of time through schedules, and induces subjects to ingest the panopticon of surveillance.[20]

In addition, pharmaceuticals are deeply implicated in the new commerce in the production of data. Students are subject to ever more digital programs in schools that capture their behavior as data. This data circulates, is sold and bought, and has value as capital even when the practical use of the data is not yet apparent.[21] The interface of the body and its affect with the body and its capital accumulation potential for multinational corporations is not lost on the largest organizations that represent the interests of these corporations. For example, the OECD has been working with human capital theorists and corporations to make affect and behavior into measurable, quantifiable metrics that can become global comparative tests in non-cognitive skills.[22] The profit potential of quantifying affect and behavior is not lost on the world's biggest toy company Lego that is working to make play-based learning into a global learning standard as it expands its education division and works to make it traditional plastic bricks interface with digital screen apps. The goal is to make play quantifiable and an education standard in forms that accord with STEM and Career and Technical Education. Lego stands to profit by making their products into necessary educational equipment for schools, districts, and nations, and by making the data they induce students to make into new capital that they can trade. Marketed as educational, Lego's toys extensively tie in with other corporate cultural products made, for example, by Disney, Marvel, and DC Comics produce and affirm heteronormative and dimorphic gendered identifications and representations whether it's a bestselling toy like the *Fast and Furious* movie franchise muscle car Lego kit or the Lego Education STEAM park with its "feminine" and "masculine" toy figures.

Preciado details how the objective of contemporary capitalist "pharmpornocographic" technology is the production of the body for capital's reproduction of the species (119). Drawing on scholarship on the commons, Preciado highlights the antagonism between, on the one hand, capital's efforts to privatize and enclose biocodes of gender and, on the other hand, the possibilities of freely distributing and sharing the biocodes of gender. By "biocodes of gender," Preciado is referring to not only the signs, symbols, and narratives of gender and sexuality but also the material technologies that make bodies including hormones, drugs, and screen technology. The enclosure of the biocodes of gender involves the private control over the material and symbolic apparatuses that make gender such as drugs, hormones, and the machinery of cultural production. The enclosure of the biocodes of gender results in the production of narrow heteronormative gender categories and the demand that individuals be slotted into preformed categories defined by the fictive grounding of gender and sex into biology.

The scholarly literature on the commons and Preciado's contribution to it raise some crucial questions about how schooling presently encloses and privatizes common wealth, common labor, and the codes and signs we hold in common *and* how schooling could be imagined to build and expand the commons. The literature on the commons explains that people labor and expend energy in collective ways that in a capitalist economy is captured for individualized and privatized benefit. For example, in Bolivia all water, including lakes, rivers, puddles, and rainwater, was enclosed and privatized when the government allowed a private company to purchase the rights to all of the nation's water. The people rebelled against the law and forced the government to reverse it. Similarly, the public schools in numerous nations have been enclosed by being privatized. Some schools, for example in Chile, the United States, and Uganda to name a few, were made into private for-profit businesses and some were subject to private management and decision-making.[23] Educators and activists have challenged these educational enclosures of the commons. Another example of enclosure of the commons is the making of genetic bio-information into private property. Critics warn of a new form of slavery. Preciado emphasizes how the industries that trade in hormones and other pharmaceuticals are invested in reproducing gender difference. For example, Preciado explains how testosterone supplements can be effective forms of contraception without the negative side effects of the common estrogen and progesterone birth control. Yet, testosterone is denied as a prescription contraception for women as it masculinizes the body. Preciado calls for common control over drugs and other technologies that allow for experimentation with the body and the production of gender.

Schools produce dimorphic gender difference through multiple rituals, practices, and meaning-making activities, from curriculum content to the gendered staffing of faculty and administrators, gendered school sports, gendered extracurricular activities and bathrooms, sex education, the denial of sex education, and mandates for or against drugs, hormones, and digital technology. The role of schools as site for the production of gendered difference is imbricated with the role of schools as a site of capital accumulation through the convergence of industries that trades in drug stimulation, visual stimulation, and data.

Imagining the School with Biocodes [of Gender] in Common

This chapter began by detailing how the rightist assault on trans people is focused on education, how it is part of a broader fascist political project, and the inadequate liberal multicultural/ progressive neoliberal response to it. It proceeded to lay out the competing views of gender and sexuality including critical constructivist ones that highlight the intersections of cultural politics and political economy of gender/sex. This discussion highlighted how the debates over gender and sexual identity are imbricated with the broader role and function of schooling including its economic, political, and cultural uses. What then would it mean to rethink schooling in forms (1) that defy gender/sex and capitalist enclosure for the purpose of producing and defending the commons, and (2) that enact critical pedagogies that foster democratic and egalitarian social relations?

The "commons" refers to the collective resources, wealth, life, and energy that people share. In capitalism, the benefits from collective energy and labor are individualized and captured by owners. In contrast, to live in common means that the benefits from collective energy, labor, and wealth are shared. Capitalist enclosure of the natural commons produces environmental disaster as seen in the fossil fuel, corporate agriculture, and mining industries. Capitalist enclosure of the knowledge commons transforms ideas into private property, as with patents, making certain "ideas"—as in the formulas for medications and vaccines—only available at a cost. Knowledge in common can be freely shared and exchanged for potential universal benefit. Capitalist enclosure makes biological information that is life itself—like genetic codes used for experiments or stem cells—into private property creating the conditions for bio-slavery and profit-based bio-control. As Preciado details, capitalist enclosure of gender and sexuality coerces people physiologically and in cultural forms that demand conformity to prescribed identity categories. This includes the application of drugs and screens, the inducement and collection of data about youth and its uses for coercive control and commerce. That is, neoliberal educational restructuring that increasingly takes digital and pharmaceutical form and that targets the bodies of students colludes with and deepens these enclosures of the commons.

Market models of education treat knowledge and curriculum as commodities rather than allowing them to be shared and freely exchanged. Corporate school reform treats the natural world as ideally mined and pillaged for private ownership rather than cultivated and stewarded for public care. It privatizes the process of maturation and socialization, making human development into business and children into product, while externalizing many of the costs onto the public, like educating the next generation of workers. Privatized public schooling expands repression, targeting the poor and particularly urban non-white youth with zero-tolerance policies, heavy police presence, and security apparatuses in schools, rigid pedagogies oriented around bodily control. The disciplinary apparatuses of coercion and control are racialized and gendered.[24] And the ideological subject formation of youth in contexts of enclosure/privatization produce forms of gender and sexuality that are conducive to capitalist accumulation and privatization. A particularly clear example of this brings us back to the start of this chapter: gender-segregated school sports.

School sports like most professional team sports teach both capitalist ideology and gender ideology. School sports such as basketball, football, and baseball teach capitalist values for quantifiable progress, competition, growth, violence, and winning at any cost, learned self-discipline, submission to the hierarchical authority of the coach (later the boss), commercialism through reference to professional sports, and exclusionary competition. School sports also teach heteronormative gender ideology such as gendered division of labor, gender segregation, masculinity defined through domination and action not to mention violent and homophobic hazing, femininity defined through spectatorship such as cheerleading, and affirmation of gendered difference on the terms of masculine forms of physicality. To put it differently, school sports represent both capitalist and gender/sex enclosure. How can these practices be either transformed or ended such that athletic endeavors foster values and dispositions of collaboration, care, collective energy for collective benefit, gender deconstruction, and sexual multiplicity? Should school sports be gender integrated? This would end the debate about trans athletes yet it would be unlikely to overcome the ways that current sports produce essentialized forms of gender through competition. Should school sports that emphasize measurement of progress through explosive masculinist violence (and brain injury) like football be ended? Should school sports in which gender is irrelevant to success (like many categories of ultra-running) be elevated? Should sports of collaboration such as climbing, be elevated for values of collective uplift? School athletics can be reimagined in ways that are on the one hand not about gender segregation and the discursive production of gender norms and on the other hand not about competition, quantification of progress, and exclusionary and individualizing social relations.

People can counter capitalist and gender enclosures and build the commons of culture, external nature, internal nature, and space. Numerous privatizations and accountability models of educational reform linked to neoliberal restructuring aim to enclose the commons of culture by positioning knowledge and learning as a process of depositing by positioning knowledge as a static thing, like a commodity. These approaches conceal the social positions, interests, and ideologies of those making truth claims. Such an enclosure of the culture commons displaces dialogic modes of pedagogy with prescriptive ones.

The teacher as a cultural actor with agency responds to existing sets of meanings and material conditions and affirms or contests them through the identifications that they produce. Teachers make the commons by expanding the dialogic modes of pedagogy, by exercising pedagogical authority to link learning to social and political forces and conditions, and by making knowledge the basis for self and social understanding and action. Preciado, building on Dianne Torr's workshops, developed precisely such forms of critical pedagogies of gender in his "drag kings" seminars.

> Dianne Torr's technique of the deconstruction of femininity and apprenticeship in masculinity depends on a theatrical analytic method, on the breaking down of learned body gestures (a way of walking, speaking, sitting, getting up, looking, smoking, eating, smiling) into basic units (distance between the legs, opening of the eyes, movement of the eyebrows, speed of the arms, fullness of the smile, etc.) and examining them in their capacity as cultural signs for the construction of gender. In a second synthetic moment, different cultural codes are rearranged to construct a different gender fiction. The goal of Dianne's workshops is to experiment physically and theatrically with the ways in which masculinity is produced by an array of performative cultural codes learned and incorporated through what Judith Butler has called "regularized and constrained repetition of norms … In order to construct my own workshops, I have learned from Diane's performative analysis of action, combined with a psychopolitical method that is closer to posttraumatic reeducation of the body and to the training of political minorities for survival, starting with gender suspicion and the elaboration of a collective narrative. There is no anatomical truth independent of the cultural and political practices of constrained repetition that lead us toward being men or women.[25]

To make the commons of culture involves situating knowledge and experience in terms of broader social, systemic, and structural forces. It also involves translating personal and private problems into public problems that demand theorization and intervention. Rejecting the individualization of self-formation in traditional forms of psychology, Preciado develops "the drag king workshops as a new practice of political therapy, part of an array of techniques of criticism, reprogramming, and psychopolitical care that we might call *queeranalysis.*"[26] How, we can consider, might school sports be subject to such queeranalysis? It is easy to imagine the implementation of such practices in schools. Take, for example, Shakespearean theater, perhaps the ultimate example of canonical curriculum, was traditionally performed in drag with males playing the female parts. Embracing this 400-year-old literary theater tradition of drag lends itself to the kind of drag king workshops in schools modeled on those developed by Preciado (or maybe playing on Virginia Woolf's 1928 novel *Orlando*, as Preciado did in his recent film, *Orlando, My Political Biography*). It could also be extrapolated to other sites in schools that produce gender such as school sports. For example, should girls learn to deconstruct, reconceptualize, and practice a different kind of gender by becoming football players?; Should boys be cheerleader drag kings? Can such projects that deconstruct normative gender simultaneously deconstruct ideologies that bolster capitalist values over humane values: quantified progress, competitive individualism, violent domination? Can educators work with students to imagine athletic programs that instead foster values of collective support and shared physical aspirations?

Struggles over knowledge, the curriculum, and the culture of schools are inextricably bound up with struggles not just over the self but also over the material spaces for schools. For example, when public schools get privatized, the decisions about what to teach and how to teach, the teacher work conditions, and teacher autonomy get removed from public control and shifted to control by interested private parties.

The past few decades of neoliberal educational restructuring—with its push for charters, vouchers, neo-voucher scholarship tax credits, and more recently digital educational privatization—represents an enclosure of educational space. For example, vouchers worsen educational resource inequality, segregating by class. Charters have been shown to expand racial segregation as well as intensifying racialized class inequality in part by pushing out English Language Learners and students with disabilities. These exacerbated educational inequalities need to be seen as adjuncts to the broader making of new walls and slums through radical economic inequality and hyper-ghettoization, mass incarceration, and the modeling of schools on prisons and the military. Increasing social and school repression has been a feature of neoliberal educational restructuring which favors repressive pedagogies and models of corporeal control.

Building the commons demands going in the other direction: making schooling the basis for freedom and autonomy as learning becomes the basis for social understanding and collective action to address public problems. The lived experiences of oppression—not just class and gender oppression but ethnic, linguistic, disability oppression—become the basis for theorizing and reconceptualizing public problems and developing interventions. Schooling becomes the basis not merely for academic preparation for more schooling or work but for social improvement and structural change.

Neoliberal educational restructuring has taken on increasingly digital, corporeal, and affective forms in the past few years. Some examples include the expansion of personalized learning, biometric pedagogies, AI reading instruction, the quantification of play for commercial purposes and making of play based learning into a global learning standard, and online apps for SEL. Both the new data extraction mode of educational privatization and the explosion of resilience discourse have sought to target the commons of internal nature in students for privatization and enclosure, blaming students for not trying hard enough when the odds of success are stacked against them.

Contrary to digital privatization, teachers can teach critical digital literacies, produce critical pedagogies using new technologies that expand the commons by linking objects to their conditions of social production and to the power relations that animate their social circulation. For example, among the most dire contemporary public problems today is the environmental crisis. Increasingly, the effects of global warming are being directly experienced. The pedagogies of control that aim to pacify consciousness and control bodies through the use of pharma and screen technology fail to relate learning to the experiences of human and natural caused disaster. Contrary to the enclosures of resilience pedagogies that demand adaptation to existing conditions, teachers can teach students to interpret their affective states, behavior, and identifications in relation to the social and political forces that produce them, making the self an object of critical analysis. Such critical analysis builds the commons by expanding student agency, allowing students to comprehend how they are being socially produced as particular kinds of prescribed subjects (gendered, raced, classed) and hence how they can use a new understanding of their experiences to formulate collective action to address the forces that produce the experience of domination and oppression of all kinds and forge themselves as different kinds of subjects. It also allows students to understand that the world was made by people and can also be unmade by people like them. As well, students can learn how pedagogical repression in the form of drugging students into attention and focus or applying digital control technologies comes at the expense of critical pedagogies, specifically because of the evacuation of meaningful experience from the process of schooling. Critical pedagogies begin with student experience and the social and cultural context. They are meaningful and motivating because they relate learning to students' prior experiences. But they also problematize prior experience, allowing students to theorize the multiplicity of taken for granted ideological meanings, rituals, and practices they have been taught.

4

Trauma Doping: Anti-Anxiety Medication and the New Trauma Education Industries

This chapter considers the drug-technology industry nexus by examining the relationship between the vast prescription of anti-anxiety drugs for students and the new technology industries justified by the discourse of trauma. Students are given anti-anxiety medications in record numbers as treatment for stress and trauma. While possibly providing short-term relief, these drug practices nonetheless obscure, medicalize, and individualize the social, economic, and cultural causes of stress and trauma. As well, the massive growth of resilience products—particularly digital ones in mindfulness, social and emotional learning, growth mindset, meditation, and grit—is justified on the physiological and trauma of poverty. These resilience products and programs do not cure either the trauma or the social conditions that justify their sales but they do generate massive profits for educational contractors while operating as instruments of corporeal control and replacing critical pedagogies that foster self and social understanding.

Trauma has become a widely used trope ranging from medical and scientific use to vast popular use. Historically, trauma referred to psychological injury involving repression that could have behavioral or physiological symptoms. For example, Freud developed psychoanalytic therapy to bring to the conscious mind repressed traumas that he thought were manifesting as neurotic or psychotic symptoms. For Freud, trauma blocked a memory but also rerouted, displaced, fragmented, and condensed it, so that it manifested in disruptions to everyday life that would reemerge as obstacles to development and sometimes maladaptive behaviors unless therapeutically reinterpreted. The meaning of trauma has evolved to refer most commonly to conscious psychological stress and its physical impacts. It has recently become central to a number of educational theories including human capital theory and trauma-informed pedagogy. These views suggest that trauma presents a blockage to the successful transmission of knowledge to the student. As well, resilience programs in grit, growth mindset, meditation, and SEL are supposed to overcome trauma through instilling self-discipline and task persistence in students or teaching techniques like breathing exercises, meditation, listening to chimes, or guided visualization.

In what follows, I first detail several social factors that have resulted in rising subjective states of anxiety and significantly increased rates of diagnosis for anxiety disorders and prescriptions for pharmaceuticals. Then I recount how human capital, trauma-informed pedagogy, and resilience programs frame the causes and solutions to trauma and anxiety in individualized and depoliticized ways that misunderstand cause and effect to put the onus for addressing social problems onto the individual. Lastly, I contrast how critical pedagogy provides a social and political mode of interpretation of experience that aims not for social control and passive depoliticized modes of learning but forms of learning that make emotional states into objects of critical analysis and a basis for critical consciousness, agency, and collective political projects.

Anxiety Rising

From 2007 to 2019, rates of youth anxiety and depression have significantly increased in the United States.[1] According to the Centers for Disease Control and Prevention (CDC), rates of diagnosis of anxiety of youth went from 5.5 percent in 2007 to 9.5 percent by 2019 rising steadily.[2] 5.8 million children were diagnosed with an anxiety disorder by 2019.[3] The most commonly prescribed youth anxiety drugs are Selective Serotonin Reuptake Inhibitors (SSRIs) and Selective Serotonin Norepinephrine Reuptake Inhibitors (SSNRIs), both of which increase the amount of neurotransmitters in the brain, anxiolytics including Benzodiazapines (Klonopin, Ativan), antipsychotics, and anti-histamines.[4] Youth diagnosed with anxiety are being widely prescribed pharmaceutical treatment but not therapy despite studies showing that anxiety is most effectively treated with a combination of pharmaceuticals and therapy.[5] The global market in anti-anxiety and depression pharmaceutical drugs is enormous and growing. It was US$8.5 billion in 2019 and projected to reach $13 billion annually by 2027 with North America representing a disproportionate share of consumption.[6] In addition there are booming markets in supplements, alternative treatments, and digital therapies.

The trend of targeting the bodies of youth to manage its affect needs to be comprehended in relation to the social factors involved in producing the subjective experience of anxiety. Rising anxiety needs to be seen in part as an effect of expanding economic, political, and social precarity. In 2018, the richest 1 percent controlled more than half of all the world's wealth while 80 percent of the global population controlled just 5 percent of wealth. "Worldwide, 50 percent of all people live on less than $2.50 a day and a full 80 percent live on less than $10 a day."[7] Extreme economic inequality has continued to worsen, with the Covid-19 pandemic significantly increasing it.

> As savage as global inequalities already were, the wealth gap widened rapidly around the world during the pandemic. Assisted by corporate bailouts, in the United States, the ultra-wealthy increased their wealth by $931 billion from March to October 2020, even as sixty million workers lost their jobs, and as poverty, hunger, and homelessness spread. Worldwide, billionaires' wealth jumped by 27 percent, to $10.2 trillion in just four months of the pandemic,

from April to June 2020, according to a report by the Swiss bank UBS, which also warned against the threat of a global uprising by the poor against the superrich.[8]

Expanding economic precarity is informing the rise of political precarity as governments appear increasingly incapable of addressing public problems. The state faces crises of legitimation as fascist Strongmen leaders rise in numerous countries promising security through identifications with domination. Neoliberal ideology plays a large role in producing economic and political insecurity as the defunding of the public caregiving roles of the state through privatizations (education, healthcare, mental health services) continues to be felt around the world. As Zymunt Bauman observed,[9] politics is experienced as local but corporate power is global in scope, resulting in challenges to collectively address public problems such as environmental crisis, the erosion of democracy, militarism and colonial violence driven by empires, and dire inequalities in wealth and income. Global corporations such as oil companies, banks, pharmaceutical companies, and weapons manufacturers successfully lobby and influence governments on a global scale. However, individuals and local political movements are hampered in their capacities to organize and act globally. In the United States, Democrats have doubled down on a neoliberal model that has proven itself a failure at addressing public problems. That is, Democrats have failed to rebuild the eviscerated social state with, for example, free public university, free public healthcare, affordable housing, the eradication of student debt, and a commitment to bring public school funding up to the levels of the most supported schools. Instead, they have continued to support obscene levels of spending on the machinery of repression and imperial control: weapons, military, and policing. Republicans, remade through right-wing populist promises of Trumpism have promised protectionism, economic nationalism, and nativism paired with a reactionary if not fascist cultural politics that scapegoats and targets minorities, women, non-heterosexuals, and immigrants while promising to radically end multiple civil liberties. Despite the promises to challenge neoliberal economic doctrine, Trump's presidency promoted privatization, appointed a billionaire cabinet, and exacerbated economic inequality, in part through tax cuts for the super-rich and corporations.

The shift from the Keynesianism of the Fordist era to the era of neoliberalism, post-Fordism, and the financialized economy marked a broader social tendency to move away from time- and labor-intensive modes of self and social control in favor of manipulating the body.[10] In the Fordist era, time- and labor-intensive forms of learned self-discipline gave way to post-Fordist modes of control dominated by corporeal coercion. In part, this represented a change in the form of capital accumulation that decreasingly required time- and labor-intensive investments in social relations conducive to labor exploitation and that increasingly required direct forms of extraction. The rehabilitative aims of the prison were replaced by locking away bodies in the increasingly privatized prison. The talk therapy of psychoanalysis gave way to the management of affect directly through the administration of pills for anxiety, depression, and so on. The capitalist aims of the school in producing docile and disciplined future workers gave way in part to more immediate forms of capital accumulation in schools. Bodies have increasingly become the locus for lucrative contracts in charter and other privatized schools, technology products, and more recently the making students into data production engines (also managed by drugs).

In addition to crises of economics and politics, there is a crisis of agency as the tools for people to make sense of and act on social and political conditions are weakened or eradicated.[11] Corporate consolidation of mass media resulted in radical declines in investigative journalism.[12] Most Americans now get their news from social media posts rather than from news sources with editorial processes. Most public policy is driven by vested interests such as lobbying with almost no legislation coming from activists and social movements.[13] Meanwhile the intellectual tools to interpret and judge claims to truth are under attack as the political right expands censorship of books, libraries, and school libraries and places gag orders on teachers, bans curriculum, and attacks critical theory.

Technology is also implicated in producing social and subjective precarity, anxiety, and depression. In 2024, the Surgeon General of the United States proposed putting medical warnings on social media. Dr. Vivek Murthy "pointed to research that showed that teens who spent more than three hours a day on social media faced a significantly higher risk of mental health problems, and that 46 percent of adolescents said social media made them feel worse about their bodies."[14] US teenagers spend 4.8 hours per day on social media sites such as YouTube, TikTok, and Instagram.

These studies are valuable but do not socially situate the conditions that give rise to such affective states. As scholars such as Byun Chul Han and Franco Berardi point out, anxiety, depression, and burnout are at epidemic levels, in part due to the ways that semio-capitalism structures time, space, and subjectivity. Berardi argues that semio-corporations aim to make the relations between people and machines flexible.[15] Consequent multitasking results in affective disorders.[16] People find no outside to labor time with email, text, messaging, and social media continuing into off hours and through the night.[17] Leisure and health become increasingly quantified through biometrics. Despite the widely perceived failure of online education for children during the pandemic, students are exposed to screens, apps, avatars, AI, and no end of digital technology in schools as well as outside of them. Berardi stresses that the finite capacities of the body and consciousness come up against the infinite flow of information that bombards people yielding pathologies.[18] Alienation is exploding in this context. As well, the unending and always failing project of projecting what Byun Chul Han calls subjects of achievement results in a sense of selfhood in which the self is constantly being measure against the quantified representation of online others.[19] Self becomes a project of always failing to get enough likes, clicks, hearts, and thumbs up. The contemporary project of becoming an always inadequate self recapitulates the logic of television advertisement in which ads simultaneously promise a dreamworld of consumption while forming viewers as lacking—lacking not just the product for sale but the dreamworld of consumption that the product represents. Social media self-formation adds to this machinery of lack-production metrics and interactive feedback in real time, amplifying the lack. The data we produce through use of digital devices is not just bought and sold but forges a consumer profile that becomes the basis for further marketing us products and lack.

The past decade has seen the intensified stoking of racial anxiety, in particular by right-wing populist and fascist political movements that have paired rhetoric of economic nationalism with white supremacist, xenophobic, nativist, and other forms of hateful expression. These movements have sought to respond to white working-class disenchantment with the unfulfilled promises of neoliberal ideology, promising to turn against trade liberalization in order to pair economic nationalism with a cultural politics of racialized revanchism. These movements have displaced structural and systemic criticism of capitalism and its destructive effects with conspiracy-oriented narratives that, for example, attack not neoliberal globalization or financialized capitalism but an anti-semitically coded "globalist agenda" enacted by a secret cabal of conspirators. In this discourse, those made most precarious by the current social order, such as migrants, are scapegoated for systemic inequalities not of their making.

School has long been adept at producing anxiety and insecurity through the system of grades and tests. The logic of the examination, as Foucault detailed as disciplinary power, sorts and sifts, compares, differentiates, normalizes, watches, and produces subjects always in a state of measuring up and knowing that they are being watched.[20] As Bourdieu contended, a major class-based achievement of schooling is to translate the unequal distribution of cultural capital and life chances within the class hierarchy into a matter of self-blame.[21] You don't have the career, job, income, meaningful work, but it's your own fault for lacking the innate ability, hard work, and perseverance in school. Allegations of deficit and laziness are levied against working-class and poor Black and brown students in urban districts, amplifying broader public discourses about race and class, capacity, and diligence. The logic of positivism is at play, translating alleged merit and talent into numbers that have an allure of disinterested objectivity and neutrality obscuring the cultural politics behind them. Augmenting feelings of inadequacy and lack, these processes are all at work in schools and are amplified by digital technology such as so-called personalized learning programs (which are not personalized) that put in place standardized curriculum, teaching to the test, and ever more frequent testing. Despite the moniker "personalized learning," such digital curriculum programs are incapable of considering students' cultures, class positions, and contexts in relation to knowledge or to make learning meaningful by relating it to both experience and the broader social world and social forces. The use of educational technology amplifies the ideology of positivism falsely, suggesting that the teaching and learning in these programs deliver neutral, disinterested, and apolitical knowledge in an ever more efficient manner. The obscuring of class- and cultural-based knowledge and ideologies redistributes blame and responsibility for social failure onto the student and away from those who actually make the curriculum and such transmissional models of pedagogy. The process of schooling becomes for those who are not represented in the official knowledge one of not just drudgery and dead time but also one in which the failures of the system are experienced as personal failures of character and capacity.

The conceptual trope of trauma needs to be comprehended in relation to the undermining of youth agency. Positivist ideology in its long-standing and newer incarnations is a major culprit in undermining students' sense of the capacity to use knowledge to understand and impact the world they inhabit. Positivist ideology treats knowledge as a collection of facts that appear to come from nowhere.[22] It disregards the subjective dimension of knowledge-creation, erring on the side of a false objectivism. For example, standardized tests disappear the person who made the test, also disappearing the class position, cultural values, ideological assumptions, and interests of the person. This disallows a student from engaging with that person and interrogating the values and assumptions behind why some truth claims are on the test and others are not, how some answers appear and others do not. The standardized test frames learning as passive reception, frames knowledge as an object that can be delivered and received. It thus undermines students' agency—that is, the sense of the capacity to interpret and use knowledge to understand the self and society in order to shape the world one inhabits. Despite the opt-out movement against excessive standardized testing and teaching to the test, some educational technologies such as personalized learning have made constant testing into the curriculum itself.

The expansion of social media use by youth is also implicated in crises of affective states. Girls in particular are suffering skyrocketing rates of anxiety, depression, and suicide in response to technologies that demand image-based normalization and comparison with others.[23] Ninety-five percent of youth aged 13–17 are using social media. A 2019 study published in *JAMA Psychiatry* found that for adolescents using social media more than three hours "may be at heightened risk of developing mental health problems, particularly internalizing problems."[24] In the past few years, anxiety and other affective states have become the focus and attention of education specialists who are promoting specific interpretations of student anxiety, depression, and other adverse states as "trauma." Such research individualizes trauma as a chemical or biological effect of the body or as a psychological problem to a bad experience. Whatever the extent of the bad experience, the treatment is also individualized through diagnosis, therapy, "work on self" (including mindfulness and meditation, for example), and sometimes medication. These means of treatment do not address the broader social context's effects on the anxious subject.

Not only are educational practices and commercial technologies producing states of anxiety, depression, and self-blame, but academic discourses are framing the subjective effects of violent social policy as causes rather than effects. Three such academic discourses are human capital theory, trauma-informed pedagogy, and resilience.

Trauma in Human Capital Discourse

Human capital theory has been developed by proponents to include a social psychological narrative about trauma and poverty. In this narrative, poverty causes trauma that can be measured physiologically as "high allostatic load."[25] Human capital theorists contend that this trauma causes a blockage to students being good consumers of knowledge. Consequently, they propose programs that supposedly treat the individual trauma but not the causes of the poverty that produce the trauma as well as all of the other social violence that poverty causes like physical and mental illness and deprivation of public and private goods and services. Human capital theorists advise "non-cognitive skills" development that will supposedly address trauma and unblock the blockages to the consumption of knowledge.

Human capital theorists endorse programs in learned self-control and control of affect and behavior. Such programs include: grit—a behaviorist training method in task persistence; SEL—programs that have students identify emotions but not their social origins in order to supposedly unblock blockages to the consumption of knowledge. They also have worked with supra-national organizations such as the OECD to develop metrics to quantitatively measure affective "non-cognitive skills."

Human capital theory was developed by the "Chicago Boys"—a group of economists who followed Milton Friedman at the University of Chicago—who formulated and promoted neoliberal ideology. Human capital theory contends that investments in education result in economic growth and development. What is most significant about human capital theory is the framing of education as a primarily economic good rather than as a political or cultural good. Human capital theory seeks to create economistic formulas that will justify the reduction of public spending on public education. One of the major fallacies of human capital theory is the assumption that education causes economic growth regardless of capital investment. Championed by Gary Becker among others, human capital theory justifies disregarding the relationship between education and its uses in the reproduction of class hierarchy.

Human capital theory stands in stark contrast with Bourdieu and Passeron's theory of cultural capital and social capital. As Bourdieu and Passeron detail, education is implicated in the reproduction of the class hierarchy through the addition of non-monetary forms of capital transmission from parents to children: cultural capital (which begins in the home)—the socially valued knowledge, tastes, and dispositions—and social capital which refers to the socially advantageous social networks made in the educational context.[26] As Bourdieu and Passeron point out, the forms of capital are convertible into each other. The theory explains how cultural advantage is reproduced and implicated in the social inertia that results in people largely staying in their class position of origin.

Human capital theory denies the cultural politics of knowledge, wrongly presuming that what is taught is class- and culturally neutral, of universal value. There is no recognition in this discourse of how the particular knowledge of ruling groups is universalized and imposed, nor on how knowledge is dynamic as it can be the basis for critique, resistance, critical consciousness, opposition, and reflective action. It also presumes a transmission model of pedagogy that Freire referred to as "Banking Education." In this view, which relies upon metaphors from the industrial economy, knowledge is made like a commodity and deposited in a student. The greater is the production and delivery, the greater the "investment" in educational development. Human capital theory has been embraced by supra-national organizations such as the World Bank which represents global banks and multinational corporations and their views of education. Human capital theory has participated in scapegoating education for the very neoliberal structural adjustment policies that have wrought havoc on the economies of nation-states in the Global South and have been imposed by the World Bank and International Monetary Fund— organizations that represent banks and multinational corporations. These policies forced nations to sell off and privatize their public infrastructure while being subjected to debt servitude from rich nations and banks.

Human capital theorists naturalize the effects of social and political decisions and conditions as beyond human agency and biologize the destructive effects of social and political decisions. In doing so the only action that can be taken by individuals to address social and political problems is on the terrain of the self—to treat individual trauma with resilience programs or therapy. Human capital theorists frame out of consideration the prospect of addressing the problems they have been creating through collective political action.

Trauma-Informed Pedagogy

Trauma-informed pedagogy is a recent educational trend that aims to instill in students learned self-control to allow for students to become unblocked receptacles of knowledge. Trauma-informed pedagogy presumes that trauma is the result of "adverse childhood experiences." It relies on the 1997 Adverse Childhood Experiences (ACEs) study which claimed that students with greater incidents of adverse childhood experiences (abuse, household challenges, neglect) would later in life suffer from higher rates of depression, drug use, disease, domestic abuse, financial instability, and low levels of academic achievement.[27] According to trauma-informed pedagogy, ACEs result in "toxic stress" which is a physiological result of excessive cortisol production. Toxic stress is said to in turn threaten learning defined through the consumption of knowledge. The solution to toxic stress is purported to be resilience programs in growth mindset, mindfulness, SEL, and meditation.

As I detail in greater length in *The Disaster of Resilience*, trauma-informed pedagogy makes a number of problematic assumptions. Among these is the assumption that adverse childhood experiences are a cause rather than an effect of structural and systemic inequality and oppression. For example, the violence of poverty and economic inequality, white supremacy, and patriarchy result in abuse, household challenges, and neglect. The ACEs study obscures the sociological patterns underlying the production of subjective precarity and violence. Had it not done this, it would be more obvious that the solution to adverse childhood experiences would be to address the social, structural, and systemic inequalities and oppressions rather than targeting the child's self-control as the solution.

To restate an example I use in *The Disaster of Resilience*, Jennifer Bashant's *Building a Trauma-informed Compassionate Classroom* provides a concise illustration of how trauma-informed pedagogy purports to work to get a student to control himself. As Bashant instructs the teacher in her book, "Your number one priority when a student is exhibiting challenging behavior is to help them become regulated." A teacher worksheet titled "Current Self-regulation Strategies" instructs the teacher to "assess the type of self-regulation strategies that the student is currently using," in order to identify "non-adaptive strategies" and teach the student adaptive strategies in their place. The worksheet lists a number of "nonadaptive strategies," including "running out of the classroom," "refusal or defiance," "silliness," "arguing and/or cursing," "physical aggression," "daydreaming," and "avoidance and/or shutting down." The teacher is supposed to examine these behaviors, determine the "purpose that each strategy serves for the student," and then work with the student to "select an adaptive strategy to replace each nonadaptive strategy." The worksheet offers the following as "adaptive strategies": "Taking deep breaths," "Listening to calming music," "Taking a walk," "Talking with a trusted adult," "Asking for help," "Exercise and/or heavy work," "Swinging/Rocking."

Part of what is remarkable and disturbing in a program such as this is that it provides no sense for how the teacher is to interpret the student's behavior. Is the student's "refusal" or "defiance" a response to the work that the teacher imposes, to the student's past trauma, or to the work being unrelated to anything that the student might find meaningful, relevant, or valuable? Is the student's "avoidance/shutting down" about some past trauma or a matter of the classroom being experienced as "dead time" because the curriculum appears decontextualized and meaningless? Is "daydreaming" or "silliness" a symptom of a past trauma or an outlet for the student's creativity which the curriculum and pedagogical approach does not allow? Is "aggression" or "running out of the classroom" a symptom of trauma or an act of opposition and resistance to an educational context that is experienced as oppressive, an imposition, or even potentially as a form of state-imposed violence against working-class and poor students and non-white students?

Bashant's program offers nothing to answer any of these crucial questions but rather assumes that in every case the student's behavior is a symptom of a past trauma. Yet, if it is a function of a past trauma, the program provides no way for the teacher to engage with the student about the traumatic experience or the immediate or broader social causes of it. Such a program provides no means for the teacher to comprehend the student behavior or relate the interpreted behavior to the proposed "adaptive strategies." However, the "adaptive strategies"—such as deep breathing or listening to soothing music—have no relationship to interpreting or acting on the situation at hand. Lastly, it is completely unclear how these advocated practices relate to student learning other than as allegedly creating conditions to make students into passive receptacles for prescribed knowledge. Whereas critical pedagogy relates learning to both student experience and broader social realities such that knowledge becomes an instrument of self and social empowerment, trauma-informed pedagogy does neither.

Resilience and the Treatment of Trauma

In reaction to the objectivism of the standards and accountability movement and its overemphasis on allegedly objective facts, resilience pedagogies have expanded over the past decade, purporting to be attentive to subjective states. SEL, growth mindset, mindfulness, meditation programs, and grit programs aim to focus on students' subjective states, their affect, emotions, and behavior. These programs are expressions of the discourse of "resilience." Resilience presumes that individuals ought to learn skills of adaptation to the existing social reality and self-control toward that end. SEL programs, for example, register students' feelings so that they can supposedly learn self-control. These programs do not teach students to theorize and comprehend what in the objective world produces the subjective feelings they experience. Nor do these programs teach students to impact the objective world with a reconceptualized subjective state allowed by theory. Instead, similarly to human capital and trauma-informed pedagogy, these programs promise to unblock emotions that get in the way of students becoming passive recipients for objectified knowledge. That is, affective states become not an object of critical analysis but rather an imposition to learned self-control in the service of transmission models of pedagogy. As an object of critical analysis, feelings can be interpreted in terms of the institutional forces, systems, and structures that produce them as well as in terms of relations of power and authority.

Meditation programs such as those championed by filmmaker David Lynch or big business Calm Classroom attempt to teach students to meditate. Proponents of meditation programs target working class and poor school districts and suggest that their programs will allow students to settle their minds and counter the stress and trauma of poverty by turning students' consciousness inward. While meditation practice has established benefits, there are a number of problems with school meditation programs. The programs are often needlessly expensive, involve the sale of unnecessary things, and are of dubious efficacy in practice. Teachers in Chicago report students ridiculing meditation program Calm Classroom that has teachers use a "Zynergy" chime appropriated from Tibetan Buddhist meditation.

These programs uncritically appropriate from religious and cultural traditions without examining the broader ideas and values from which the practices developed. For example, extracting meditation from Buddhism, such programs dispense with the philosophy of non-attachment to desire. Instead, they turn meditation into a technique for personal effectiveness and an adjunct to "Banking

Education." Perhaps most significantly, meditation education programs ask students to turn their focus away from the objective world that produces their experience and emotion and instead turn inward and focus on breathing without thinking. Students who are living in communities beset by the ill effects of poverty and racist organizations of urban space and their psychological impacts would benefit from being able to comprehend their experiences and feelings in relation to the broader forces and institutions that produce them. The change to consciousness through such interpretation can be the basis for educational and social projects to challenge the forces and institutions from which said experiences emerge.

SEL, mindfulness, play-based learning, and growth mindset programs have largely become the content of for-profit digital programs in schools. As such these programs in managing affect are a large and lucrative industry that merges corporeal control with the mining of the self and body for commercial opportunities in contracting arrangements and data production.

A widely adopted mindfulness digital product is Class Dojo which is a social media application that allows for the disciplinary surveillance of students as well as teachers. Teachers take photos and videos of students in school to share with parents. Class Dojo does not charge schools for the service but it profits by selling pay for fee services in mindfulness to parents. These mindfulness programs contain, for example, cartoons of a character who puts his anger—referred to as "the beast"—in a box and has it float away, lifted by helium balloons. The program has students identify feelings but not examine what produced those feelings. Instead, they are asked to imagine the feelings disappearing. Such an approach to emotion is of dubious efficacy as therapy as it offers no means of interrogating what social conditions produce the emotion such that the meaning and impact of the emotion can be comprehended and the interpretation can be the basis to do something about what produces the emotion.

As I have detailed in *The Alienation of Fact* and *The Disaster of Resilience,* Lego and the Lego Foundation have been developing with the OECD metrics for quantifying affect in the form of play-based learning. The Lego Foundation has been promoting play-based learning as a quantified measure of affect and promoting play-based learning as treatment for trauma suffered by migrants. The Denmark-based toy company Lego is the world's largest toy company, historically produced plastic bricks. Though Legos were originally used for free play, over time they have increasingly sold sets that are prescriptive, requiring children to follow a recipe to make the toy. The kits have become increasingly commercially tied to blockbuster film, television, and gaming cultural products such as Marvel and DC. More recently Lego Education has developed STEM kits that interface plastic block kits with digital apps. As Lego works with the OECD to make play a quantified measure of "non-cognitive skills," it develops products that allow for the making and processing of data. What is at stake in this project for Lego is massive profit potential. However, the social and educational stakes include the redefinition of play from being about imagination and creativity to being prescriptive, the capture of student affect and activity for potentially commercially lucrative data manufacture, and expanded surveillance. Lego justifies and legitimates these activities by claiming that they are helping traumatized migrants adapt to their new homes.[28]

Some of the largest and most influential promoters of educational privatization have pivoted to the new terrain of digital educational profiteering specifically by investing in digital resilience products in SEL, mindfulness, and growth mindset. These for-profit digital emotional resilience products follow the logic of human capital theory that presumes trauma is a blockage to the efficient consumption of knowledge. The New Schools Venture Fund was a major financial backer of educational privatization in the form of charter schools. As for-profit education has become increasingly digital, it has invested in for-profit digital companies many of which sell SEL programs. Centervention's ZooU is an example, purporting to teach students social interaction by having them not interact with other students or adults but by playing animated games with tests in "appropriate" affective responses to the situations in the cartoons.

From Resilience and Trauma to Critical Pedagogy

Critical analysis of subjective states makes an object of analysis of internalized values, assumptions, and ideologies that are experienced as emotion. As well, critical pedagogy encourages situating feelings and experiences in terms of broader social tendencies, social antagonisms, and contradictions that install themselves in the subject through processes of identification. A starting point for such analysis is to identify what are perceived as personal problems and to engage in dialog about what causes them. The key move is, as C. Wright Mills described, translating personal problems into public problems.[29] This involves making an object of analysis of what one subjectively experiences, situating it in terms of broader material and symbolic structures, systems, and forces that inform and produce it. This also requires situating the self within the social that produces it by examining of the economic, political, cultural, and pedagogical forces at work in forming emotions. There is a necessary element of unlearning habits of self-interpretation taught by, for example, the self-help industries, pop psychology, and popular culture that mis-frame the origins of emotion in the self rather than in society. In schooling, SEL, mindfulness, and meditation programs have participated in mystifying the social origins of emotion by asking students to be aware of their emotions but not examine what socially produces them. Such programs themselves can be an object of critical analysis in schools, allowing students to comprehend how and why these programs mis-frame feelings and opening an analysis of what in the broader social world produces those feelings. Such analysis can involve questions as to who wins and loses from particular interpretive frameworks for emotion, who benefits financially and culturally from some framings rather than others.

A crucial difference between how trauma is understood by human capital, trauma-informed pedagogy, and resilience programs on the one hand and, on the other hand, critical pedagogy has to do with the different assumptions about the meaning of knowledge and curriculum. The collection of trauma programs presumes that trauma gets in the way of consuming knowledge that has no particular meaning to the student's sense of self. Trauma is treated as a bottleneck, obstacle, or imposition to the aim of filling the student with knowledge. In this way, both trauma and knowledge are alienated from the student's experience. In contrast, critical pedagogy makes traumatic experience and indeed all experience the basis for critical problem posing to examine the social conditions that created it. As well, critical pedagogy does not position knowledge as an alienated thing to be deposited whose value is grounded in the authority of the teacher or technology. Instead, it fosters, in students, habits of investigation to examine the social authority, social positions, interests, values, and ideologies of those asserting claims to truth. While trauma programs ask students to register their emotions in order to put them away, overcome them through breathing or visualization, critical pedagogy asks students to understand their emotions, the origins of their emotions outside of themselves and the power relations and politics behind their emotions. Part of what is significant about this difference is that while trauma programs reassert the self as origin of what is experienced as a problem, critical pedagogy helps a student comprehend that their emotions are to a great extent a social product, generated by larger economic, political, and cultural forces. By misdirecting student to ignore and misattribute the causes of their emotions, trauma programs also participate in undermining the power that students have to identify the social and political sources of oppression and develop with other students and teachers the political projects to act to change those forces.

Critical pedagogy fosters, in students, self and social understanding and agency. Whether they are pharmaceutical or behavioral, approaches to trauma that target students' bodies for control ought to be seen as a kind of violence committed against students in that they actively undermine the capacities of students to better understand themselves or the society they inhabit and the power relations producing the oppression they experience. Arguments in defense of drugging students into coping or training students for adaptation in the name of "academic achievement" depend on denying the systematic making of precarious social conditions and inequality that form and inform anxiety, depression, and trauma. Such arguments are arguments for maintaining ignorance and self-blame for the effects of conditions not made by students.

5

Race, Drugs, and the School to Prison Pipeline

This chapter explores the contradictions in the newest iteration of radically disparate treatment of drugs for different populations. The chapter makes the case for decriminalizing youth and expanding efforts to teach the social, political, and cultural causes for the uses of drugs in and out of schooling including the uses of drugs to stimulate interest in meaningless, decontextualized knowledge and the uses of drugs to counter the stimulation deficit of non-screen time. The first section details the legalization of formerly illegal drugs. The second section discusses the continuation of the racialized war on drugs, particularly as schools are implicated in it. It also discusses how the decriminimalization and then recriminalization of pill-based opioids (the opioid epidemic) relates to the legacy of the drug war and the possibilities of popular movements to educate the public about drugs differently than has been done in the past. The chapter explores the contradiction between legalization and criminalization of drugs and the ways that both are implicated in reproducing the racialized class structure in the interest of new profit schemes.

Legalization

We are seeing radical changes in the use and acceptability of drugs. Though historically connected to what got labeled as the "moral failing" of inner cities and minority populations, formerly illicit and disparaged drugs such as cannabis, psylocibin mushrooms, and other hallucinogens have been legalized, decriminalized, mass marketed, and celebrated in mass media as cures for addiction and trauma and increasingly are framed as integral to programs for wellness and health. Meanwhile, a movement has grown to bring down legal pharmaceutical purveyors of opioids such as the Sackler family and Purdue Pharma for conspiring to make the lucrative opioid epidemic that has resulted in millions of overdose deaths. This movement has made popular that drug addiction is a social not an individual problem and has sought redress for those who have forced addiction onto people in order to profit from the addiction. At the same time, Black and brown students in the poorest schools continue to be targeted by the school to prison pipeline with expulsions and criminal charges for illegal drugs and a profitable industry in juvenile justice contracting.

Cannabis, which in the United States was until 2024 classified as a highly punishable schedule 1 drug, was decriminalized by ten states in the 1970s and legalized by some states for non-medical use starting from 2012. As of this writing, twenty-four states have legalized non-medical cannabis use, and it is on the ballot in multiple other states. The cannabis industry in the United States is worth roughly $40 billion a year. In the spring of 2024, the federal government of the United States reclassified cannabis from being a schedule I drug—the only classification that cannot by prescribed by a doctor. Cannabis has widespread medical use as an anti-emetic drug used in conjunction with chemotherapy and radiation therapy. It is widely used in the treatment of sleep disorders and anxiety. Due to being classified as schedule 1, research in the United States was stopped for decades. By being reclassified as a schedule 3 drug in 2024, cannabis corporations are able to get tax benefits, but those imprisoned on cannabis related federal convictions will not be freed (except in Maryland).

Recent attempts to mainstream formerly illicit drugs have questioned the common sense that such drugs only give benefits to individuals in the form of pleasure and self-indulgence. In the book and documentary film *How to Change Your Mind*, Michael Pollan details how psychedelic drugs such as LSD (acid) and psilocybin mushrooms are being researched for their potential to treat Obsessive Compulsive Disorder (OCD), addiction, eating disorders, depression, anxiety, and to treat terminally ill patients to cope with their approaching deaths.[1] The book and film explain scientific accounts of how psychedelic drugs affect the parts of the brain (the default mode network) that are responsible for forming a sense of self. "Nodes in the default network are thought to be responsible for autobiographical memory, the material from which we compose the story of who we are, by linking our past experiences with what happens to us and with projections of our future goals."[2] Psychedelics decrease blood flow and oxygen to the parts of the brain associated with the default mode network. In this account, the experience of tripping on psychedelics results, says Pollan, in a "dissolving of self," a sense of being able to objectify the self and maintain autobiographical narratives of the self, and consequently, a feeling of connection to the totality of the world and others. In this view on psychedelics, the stories we have about ourselves break down and can be denaturalized and questioned. In this account, the default mode network in mental illnesses of control (OCD, eating disorders, PTSD) is characterized by a maladaptive response mechanism: excessive internal reflection on the self, and the repetition of narratives of the self. Psychedelics supposedly interrupt the internal reflection and the narratives. A neuroscientist Pollan interviews, who studies the effects of psychedelics on the brain, reports, "A lot of mental illnesses appear to be defensive reactions to uncertainty."[3] An illness such as an eating disorder provides certainty, assuredness, control, but, by breaking down the default mode network, tripping disassembles the "sense of self" and allows one to see things differently, decontextualizing, putting in perspective, recontextualizing and connecting the self to all other things.

The film likens the state of wonder of tripping to the wonderment children have at the novelty of first experiencing things. "Psychedelics push back against the maladaptive defense mechanism." Following the use of these psychedelics, patients report cured of these various "illnesses of control." Pollan interviews a neuroscientist, Kevin Carhart-Harris.

> Carhart-Harris suggests that the psychological "disorders" at the low-entropy end of the spectrum are not the result of a lack of order in the brain but rather stem from an excess of order. When the grooves of self-reflective thinking deepen and harden, the ego becomes overbearing ... Carhart-Harris believes that people suffering from a whole range of disorders characterized by excessively rigid patterns of thought—including addiction, obsessions, and eating disorders as well as depression—stand to benefit from the "ability of psychedelics to disrupt stereotyped patterns of thought and behavior by disintegrating the patterns of [neural] activity upon which they rest ... This is where psychedelics come in. By quieting the default mode network, these compounds can loosen the ego's grip on the machinery of the mind, "lubricating" cognition where before it had been rusted stuck.[4]

In addition to the use of psychedelics for medical psychiatric treatment, the book and film detail the widespread practice of "microdosing" hallucinogens to treat depression but also to inspire creativity and personal productivity for work. The film suggests that psychedelics, which first took off in the Bay area, inspired the nascent computer industry in Silicon Valley, fostering creativity and breakthroughs in technical scientific thinking. Coders used psychedelics, and the film suggests that the very connectivity of the internet may have been inspired by the sense of connectivity that psychedelic drugs provide.

What is particularly striking in recent movements to legalize psychedelics is how their earlier use for spiritual enlightenment, political movements, seeking, escape, recreation, and social connection are transformed in the much more instrumental, individualized, and market-oriented use of the drugs. Microdosing aims for personal efficacy and productivity. Macrodosing becomes rationalized as a medical psychological tool for more impactful and shorter duration treatment for mental illness. Pollan's film recounts the ways that psychedelics were invented in the case of LSD (by Albert Hoffman in Switzerland for Sandia) and discovered in long spiritual use by indigenous spiritual leaders in Mexico, Central America, and South America. Traditional uses of psychedelics were integrated into religious ceremony, ritual, and community spaces. That is, they were collective and meaningful in ways that comprehended the self as part of the larger social and natural and supernatural world. Prior to the discovery and popularization of psychedelics in the 1950s and 1960s psychedelics were implicated in resistance to European colonial, religious, and labor impositions. In contrast, scientific, military, and CIA research on the uses of psychedelics as treatment for mental illness or bioweapon expanded from the 1950s through the 1960s and represented instrumental and individualized use of psychedelics for state and corporate power. At this time the widespread availability and use of hallucinogenic drugs became a part of and influenced the political countercultural movements including especially the antiwar movement. Psychedelics facilitated and had an affinity with a counterculture that valued questioning the social order and the self, that valued collectivity, connectedness, experience, process, nature, genuine democracy, and holism. The counterculture was met with conservative reaction that sought to reassert values of conformism, obedience to authority, and the domination of society by business.[5] From the 1970s to the 2000s a war on drugs lumped together dangerous narcotics such as heroin and cocaine with relatively safe drugs such as psychedelics and cannabis. Psychedelics were rendered highly illegal in reaction to the addiction and destruction of narcotic abuse but also the questioning, sense of collectivity and connectedness, and countercultural inspiration that appeared as a threat to the social order to many including the occupants of the White House.

In 1971, President Richard Nixon launched his "War on Drugs," declaring in a press conference that drug addiction was "public enemy number one." The drug war targeted not only addictive narcotics but also users of non-addictive drugs such as cannabis and psychedelics with harsh criminal penalties, incarcerating more people than any other industrialized nation.[6] Also, it launched a racialized global investment in the industries of repression to fight drugs not by curbing demand but rather by targeting supply. It classified non-addictive substances that had promising medical and psychological use such as cannabis and psychedelics as schedule I drugs punishable at the greatest levels. Subsequent administrations maintained or increased funding for the drug war, subsidizing vast increases in policing and military exports to foreign regimes. The drug war justified massive public subsidies for the weapons industry. Since Nixon's announcement, the United.States has spent at least a trillion US dollars on the drug war.[7] In the 1980s minimum drug sentencing guidelines were put in place with a 100 to 1 greater punishment for smokable crack cocaine as opposed to powdered cocaine. This resulted in grossly disproportionate criminal prosecution of Black and brown people. US mass incarceration swelled to 2.3 million with 77 percent of inmates being Black or brown.

Criminalization

As the racialized and class-based drug war was continuing, including particularly harsh sentences for narcotics possession and sales, Purdue Pharma, owned by the Sackler family, launched a potent, time-release narcotic pain pill Oxycontin. Purdue Pharma influenced the Food and Drug Administration (FDA)'s passage of a drug that was essentially heroin in a pill, aggressively marketed the drug to doctors, and misrepresented the addictiveness of the highly addictive drug as non-addictive. Purdue inspired the development of pain clinics and the mass prescribing of the drug, incentivized its salespeople to influence doctors and clinics to prescribe these pills not just to more patients but in higher dosages. This increased the risks of both overdose deaths and addiction that would in time lead to high risk of overdose. Shortly after its release, addiction, abuse of the drug by crushing and snorting or shooting it, and overdose deaths skyrocketed and became known as the "opioid epidemic." The opioid epidemic hit white rural working-class areas of the United States hard though the destruction caused by the drug was extremely widespread.

The Sackler family amassed a multibillion-dollar fortune by making highly addictive narcotics widely prescribed and consumed. Many people who became addicted to Oxycontin and Vicodin, when such prescriptions were cut off by doctors, turned to illegal dealing of these same drugs and illegal street narcotics such as heroin and fentanyl to avoid the pain and suffering of withdrawal. The Sackler family used public relations tactics of donating works of art to museums around the world and publicized their name with philanthropy. As annual deaths from overdoses in the United States passed 100,000 per year activists against the opioid epidemic publicized the profiteering of the Sackler family and Purdue Pharma by staging protests at museums and demanding the removal of the Sackler name and prosecution of the company.[8] These efforts were successful in publicizing the causes of the opioid epidemic, inspiring investigations of corporate practices, winning litigation which placed blame on the corporate profiteers, and galvanizing public support for government action to regulate pharmaceutical companies and addictive narcotic painkillers.

School to Prison Pipeline

The school to prison pipeline refers to the high rates of student expulsions of Black students. These higher rates of suspensions and expulsions from school result in high rates of school dropouts. Non-completion of high school results in youth having limited work opportunities, lower rates of pay, and a greater likelihood of involvement with illicit economies, including especially the drug trade. The school to prison pipeline disproportionately targets Black and brown youth by the juvenile justice system with high rates of continuity from juvenile to adult criminal prosecution, incarceration, and surveillance. According to the American Civil Liberties Union, Black students are suspended and expelled three times more than white students, and students expelled or suspended are three times more likely to be brought into the juvenile justice system the following year.[9] Research shows that exclusionary school policy results in greater incidence of youth drug use.

> 11 years of data from 4,800 schools and more than 4,950,000 students in California ... found that the prevalence of exclusionary school discipline (suspension and expulsion) and school-based police contact predicted higher school levels of binge drinking, drinking, smoking, using cannabis, using other drugs, and violence/harassment. They found also that the prevalence of school discipline also predicted lower levels of reported community support, feeling safe in school, and school support.

"Our findings are surprising to nobody who has been on the front lines of the fight against the mass criminalization of kids, especially in communities that have faced systematic disinvestment in social infrastructure and enormous investments in policing," says Prins, an assistant professor of epidemiology and sociomedical sciences.[10]

The authors of the study comment on the ways that the investments in repression undermine the potential to address historical public problems experienced as personal problems, writing, "heavy investments in school securitization and policing divert resources from school and community supports and services that might address the root causes of student disciplinary and health problems." The root causes of student disciplinary and health problems include racialized poverty and economic inequality, historical disinvestment in education, housing, healthcare, and other public goods and services as well as private disinvestment in poor communities. They also include forms of schooling that are meaningless, decontextualized, standardized, and disregarding of student subjectivity, culture, ideology, and class position.

The most recent study of the US Sentencing Commission examined incarceration trends from 2017 to 2021. The statistics on drug prosecutions by race show significantly higher rates of imprisonment for non-white vs. white males.

> Among males sentenced for a drug trafficking offense, the Commission found that each demographic group was less likely to receive a probation-only sentence when compared to White males. Specifically, Black males were 35.2 percent less likely, Hispanic males were 33.8 percent less likely, and Other race males were 26.8 percent less likely to receive a probation-only sentence.[11]

Taken together the recent decriminalization and legalization of formerly illegal drugs and the continuing racialized class school expulsions of youth and racialized prosecution disparities demonstrates a pattern of racially differentiated decriminalization and continuing racial targeting. The pattern cannot be comprehended just from the vantage point of disparate racial treatment within the criminal justice system. Rather, another pattern emerges when considering the processes of racialized capital accumulation and the social and cultural reproduction of the conditions of capitalist production. To put it differently, it is necessary to consider how the decriminalization and popularization of certain drugs like psychedelics and cannabis relate to the broader political economy, cultural politics, and politics of the era. In turn it is necessary to comprehend the pattern of continuing racialized prosecutions in terms of the same broader forces and tendencies.

Mass incarceration's relationship to political economy has to do in part with the racialized warehousing of surplus labor population. As William I. Robinson argues, crises of capital accumulation in financialized capitalism result in surpluses of capital and a difficulty of capital to find places to invest.[12] Mass incarceration keeps millions out of the labor force, artificially suppressing the unemployment rate. Mass incarceration also becomes a means of racialized superexploited labor profiteering in various prison industries, from forprofit prisons to the contracting and labor arrangements done by corporations in prisons. Prisoners who are disproportionately Black are paid pennies on the dollar in often-hazardous work conditions that are not covered by labor laws. Hundreds of millions of dollars are earned by major corporations such as McDonald's and Coca Cola while in some states prisoners are forced to do unpaid hard labor on plantations.[13]

Mass incarceration's relationship to political economy also has to do with the repression and political exclusion of racialized poor subjects. Financialized capitalism relies on greater coercion than did industrial capitalism. This takes form as debt servitude, the enforcement of copyright, and rent holding are central to the economies of the "core."[14] For nations in the periphery, particularly in the Global South, a logic of racialized extraction plays an outsized role in providing the rare earth minerals that are crucial components to the electronic devices used in the core for moving around money and symbols.[15]

Investment opportunities are created by destruction and targeting hitherto uncommercialized aspects of the lifeworld. For example, in 2024 Porto Alegre, Brazil, suffered a devastating storm. The mayor contracted infamous disaster "rebuilding" consultants Alvarez & Marsal to rebuild. The same Alvarez & Marsal was hired to rebuild the predominantly Black New Orleans public schools following Hurricane Katrina in 2005. They participated in the firing of all the New Orleans public school teachers, the dismantling of their unions, and the privatization of the entire district. Another example: the disaster of Covid-19 justified the massive rollout of digital online teaching technology at every educational level. Even as online distance learning technology was widely perceived as a disaster for early childhood and elementary education, following the pandemic the use of digital technology in the classroom and time spent on screens are vastly greater than that before the pandemic. Moreover, the digital technologies of repression and security in schools from biometric devices to surveillance particularly target working-class and poor students, representing investments in racialized control rather than investments in resources for engaged intellectual and educational development. The winners are the technology companies and sellers of digital curriculum products, security products, and SEL products that are sold through the use of technology. The losers are the students who are subject to numbing pedagogies of repression that offer little in the way of the intellectual tools to interpret the self and society or to collectively intervene to transform social conditions. The newest forms of educational privatization and digital technologies of surveillance and control disproportionately target working-class and poor non-white students in schools in communities subject to public and private disinvestment.

The Mis-framing of Drug Legalization and Racialized Incarceration

The films, books, and popular discourse about the legalization of psychedelic drugs do not frame the drugs as emancipatory and potentially socially and politically transformative. That is, drug legalization is not framed by proponents as being about questioning social relations and power relations. Rather, drugs are most often depicted as instruments for professional-class labor efficiency and working-class pacification. Microdosing is framed medically as either a potentially more effective pharmaceutical to anti-depressants or a means of greater worker efficiency by inspiring creativity and enhancing attention in the workplace. Macrodosing is framed not as a means of questioning the society and imagining a better society but rather as a better pharmaceutical treatment for OCD, trauma, and eating disorders. Treatment for Post-Traumatic Stress Disorder (PTSD) for veterans with LSD and mushrooms is framed not about comprehending the militarism and imperialism that produce the war and trauma but about curing the trauma with a drug to work on the body. Treatments of OCD, eating disorders, and other "illnesses of control" do not address the social experience of the diseases in terms of the broader structures and systems that produce social insecurities as they are lived and experienced individually. For example, financialized capitalism produces economic insecurity and political insecurity by the systematic undermining of democracy and support for authoritarianism, as well as cultural insecurity by eroding intellectual tools to make sense of the society and enable political agency. The precarity produced by these and other social forces is lived and experienced as individual problems and shortcomings. The psychedelics treatment movement does not, for the most part, engage with the social and political formation of pathology.

In accordance with the coercive tendencies of financialized capitalism, psychedelics promise to bypass subjectivity and consciousness and largely work directly on the body. The self-management of affect, anxiety, and depression, through benzodiazepine or selective serotonin reuptake inhibitors, takes priority over time- and labor-intensive modes of self-modulation such as talk therapy. Similarly, the self-management of inattention is primarily dealt with via amphetamines rather than with socially engaged critical pedagogies that make learning meaningful and relevant by relating it to experience and culture while making knowledge an instrument for self and social understanding and intervention. Likewise, popular framings of psychedelic treatments position the drugs as a kind of magical, mystical instrument with a physiological impact that improves self-knowledge and self-esteem. What is glaringly absent from contemporary discourse on psychedelics is a recognition of the inevitably ideological dimensions of the self before and after the psychedelic trip. This is not to deny the biological bases for mental illness but rather to point out the extent to which mental illnesses become expressed through culture, language, concepts, and ideology and only become formally recognized illnesses within particular historical cultural epochs that give them intelligibility. ADHD frames a shortage of attention as a problem in a society that demands certain kinds of attention from certain people—namely, young people expected to submit to the authority of the teacher and later the boss in an economy preparing to extract profit from a disciplined labor force that has learned to submit to wage labor. "The diseases of control" need to be addressed by being reframed through the social tendencies that make them intelligible. Crises of attention, obsession, compulsion, trauma, and consumption are functions of a society in which corporations are vying to grab and manipulate attention 24/7 through the most sophisticated technologies while making us obsess over having ever more objects, controlling others, consuming, improving, shaping, and regulating our bodies, and fantasizing about violent domination. It is certainly possible to imagine the use of psychedelic therapy that brings together self and social analysis.

The narratives of self that psychedelics allow to be denaturalized and questioned are social products. These narratives are the consequence of the process of identification with cultural products. Take, for example, eating disorders and body dysmorphia expressed through the body-modification practices of anorexia, bulimia, or the sport of bodybuilding. These are usually intricate practices of food denial and calorie burning, binging and purging, or massive muscle building via complicated eating, training, and drug-taking regimens. Such practices depend upon not just identification with a particular kind of body, thin or enormous. They also depend upon the ideological dreamworld within which such body ideals are produced, reproduced, circulated, and consumed in the form of representations. It is not a coincidence that the incident of body dysmorphia is vastly greater in consumer economies characterized by diseases of consumer excess (e.g., obesity, heart disease) than in societies characterized by scarcity.

Critical Pedagogy and Drugs

Psychedelic drugs denaturalize lived experience and perception, allowing users to question their assumptions about the world and about the self and to question the process by which individuals come to knowledge. Similarly, social philosophy and critical theory allow people to denaturalize experience and perception and question assumptions about self and society and the process of knowledge formation. While drugs estrange experience facilitating questioning, drugs do not necessarily invite questioning of power, politics, and ideology. Social philosophy and critical social theory, on the other hand, make the crucial move of situating or contextualizing social phenomena in relation to broader social tendencies, structures, and forces. By situating experience in terms of the broader social forces that produce or inform experience, experience is not just recontextualized but reconceptualized in ways that have an explanatory power. This means that the estrangement effected by critical theory gives a person the capacity to comprehend how the self is socially formed. It also provides insights as to how the self can form the society in question. Psychedelics may estrange natural reality, opening up important questions about assumptions underlying it. However, they do not necessarily provide insights about social causes behind the experience of natural reality. Nor do they, on their own, provide tools of interpretation and judgment honed from generations of scholarship, intellectual work, and traditions of thought about, for example, political economy, cultural politics, ideology, political theory, or pedagogy.

A Hopeful Development

The school to prison pipeline is often understood in ways that delink the problem from the interests and ideologies animating it. Such an approach aims to reform excessive discipline and criminalization without addressing why such racialized state violence exists or whom it serves. However, in 2024 the first African American governor of Maryland, Wesley Moore, pardoned 175,000 low-level cannabis convictions. Maryland Attorney General Anthony Brown connected disparate conviction and sentencing to the historical legacy of racial capitalism stating:

> Data uncontrovertibly shows that Black and Latino and white Americans use cannabis at the same rate, yet Black and Latino Americans are arrested, charged and convicted at

higher rates. Plainly put, the enforcement of cannabis laws has not been color blind; it's been unequal treatment under the law. ... Maryland is a work in progress. The shackles of slavery, though physically removed, left an indelible mark on our state and our nation. The promise of Reconstruction was replaced by Jim Crow laws that stripped free Black people of our rights and treated us like second-class citizens. After the Civil War, instead of freedom, we experienced the emergence of the convict leasing system, that exploited Black labor under the guise of punishment. Our current reality of disproportionate arrests and convictions are the residuals of slavery. The war on drugs was a war on communities of color. The data shows the deeply rooted bias in drug-related arrests and sentencing. Cannabis convictions for hundreds of thousands of people here in Maryland were scarlet letters, modern-day shackles. This morning, I can almost hear the clanging of those shackles falling to the floor with your pardon this morning, Governor. Thank you.[16]

Moore and Brown link the history of disparate criminal punishment to the changing legacy of racialized class exploitation. Their ethical leadership serves as a powerful example of how public officials can take bold action for social justice and educate the public about the problem they address as they address it. Their action owes in part to the long-standing efforts of scholars and activists such as Angela Davis, Michelle Alexander, Ruth Gilmour, Henry Giroux, and many others who have written extensively on the racialized punishing state. The educational relationships between this punishing state and those it has harmed demanded such remedies. In addition to the scholarship and activism that works to transform the public mind, critical pedagogies can foster critical consciousness. They can do so by teaching about the historical, political, cultural, political, economic, and ethical dimensions of the school to prison pipeline and the causes of legal and illegal drug usage, including the interests and ideologies animating them.

Tripping for Theory, Tripping on Theory

Psychedelics allow for what we think we experience as natural reality to be denaturalized, thereby calling into question both reality and our perception of it. Theory allows people to question the values, assumptions, and ideologies undergirding claims to truth and concepts. Theory allows people to situate experience in terms of broader social structures, systems, and institutions to comprehend the broader forces producing experiences of oppression. It also allows people to reconceptualize what are experienced as individual problems as social problems. Theory allows people to ruthlessly criticize existing realities and imagine alternatives. Theory enables people to not just solve problems but to take apart and recast problems as well as to develop solutions beyond that which is given by common sense. All of this conceptual work creates the conditions for collective action to address the forces that produce oppressive experience—that is, theory is integral to reflective action. Reflective action and thoughtful participation are preconditions for public discourse and the process of making and remaking a democratic society.

The contemporary trend of turning to both legal and illegal drugs to modify the body as a means of accommodating the self to existing realities is a deeply problematic trend. While drugs might provide some form of temporary comfort or solace in the midst of worsening economic, political, and cultural conditions, they do not on their own facilitate either understanding or critical analysis of social realities. Consequently, they do not necessarily facilitate the capacity to collectively act on and shape the conditions one faces. My point is not to moralize against the use of drugs but to highlight their limitations in some of the things that proponents of psychedelics say they want to do. For example, psychedelics do not on their own facilitate analysis of how the self is socially formed rather than being autonomous. Thus, psychological treatment with psychedelics on its own or paired with individualistic kinds of therapy won't necessarily move beyond locating personal problems in the self as opposed to in the society. Critical theoretical traditions allow one to comprehend better how society is structured but also how the self is structured by society. Such social interpretations of personal problems allow a person to reject tendencies of much psychology to norm, induce self-blame, or mistakenly think that speaking the "truth of oneself" can lead to liberation. On the contrary, a social interpretation of self allows a person to comprehend the agents of domination and potentially work to challenge them. As well, critical pedagogy does a number of things beyond the hopes of proponents such as addressing the social causes of what is subjectively experienced. Drugs, like many other experiences (like travel and physical training), may inspire enchantment, foster wonder, interrupt the banal and quotidian. But theory can re-enchant the world as well. Theory is crucial for resisting and ending the school to prison pipeline by providing the intellectual tools to better interpret what values, assumptions, ideologies, and interests undergird the practices that keep the pipeline going. Theoretical traditions facilitate understanding of the social forces and structures, cultural politics and concepts behind the seemingly commonsensical structuring of the everyday. Theory allows people to formulate better questions and imagine prior unimaginable solutions.

A critical pedagogy of drugs needs to bring together critical educational practices, including theorization, with social movements that aim to end the school to prison pipeline and the racialized disparate criminal drug prosecutions. It also needs to shift the conversation about and uses of both legal and illegal drugs to consider how the changing of consciousness cannot be conceived of as being about manipulating bodies by manipulating chemicals. Instead, the use of drugs needs to be considered in relation to broader questions about how social pathologies produce individual pathologies and how freeing the self through acts of interpretation and social intervention may be aided by drugs but cannot be an effect of drugs alone. A critical pedagogy of drugs needs to help students comprehend why people turn to practices of self-anaesthetization rather than critical engagement with oppressive realities, historical analysis of how drug wars and the legacies of criminalization have furthered material and symbolic interests of some over others, and serious investigations into the varieties and politics of physical pleasure. Students need critical social and educational theory to comprehend what has been done to the self by society in a systematic and structural way and how one has been educated into a particular consciousness.

Conclusion: Enchanting Education for Democratic Affect or Getting Kids Hooked on Theory

The five chapters sought to situate the drug–attention–education nexus in terms of the need for critical pedagogy and critical theory to counter the material pillage of schools and students and to counter the ideologies and affects of control. In the preceding chapters I made the case for teaching the theoretical mediation of experience as a counter to the capitalist pillage of the lifeworld of youth. I did so by considering how screens and drugs replace capitalist cultures of disenchantment with seductive bio stimulation. The affective promises of collective agency and democracy found in critical educational practice and the power of theory provide compelling and enchanting promises that can take students out of the deadlock of the drug-attention industrial complex.

In *The Dialectic of Enlightenment*, Max Horkheimer and Theodor Adorno develop Max Weber's argument that modern rationalization and bureaucracy disenchant the world.[1] Science allows for the mastery and control of nature and the displacement of mythological modes of interpretation such as religion or magic. Horkheimer and Adorno detail how Enlightenment rationality prioritizes not just scientific method but values of totality, unity, exchange, the appropriation of difference into sameness, the quantification of everything, the imposition of positivist ideology, and the mastery and control of nature.[2] Horkheimer and Adorno argue that not only does the development of Enlightenment rationality shred prior mythological understandings and disenchant the world, but that Enlightenment rationality introduces new myths and forms of irrationalism. Horkheimer and Adorno, writing in exile from Nazi Germany, were particularly concerned with the problem of how Germany, one of the most technologically advanced, culturally sophisticated, and democratic nations, could fall prey to myths such as the Teutonic nationalist and racial eugenic myths of Nazi fascism. That is, how could "civilization" evolve into "barbarism."

There are some contemporary examples of how today the logic of Enlightenment rationality transforms into myth and "barbarism." Take for example, capitalist development and the environment. Capitalism is premised on unlimited economic growth, production, and consumption, the development of ever more technologies to master nature, and the exploitation of nature and human labor. This trajectory is now widely recognized to be unsustainable for the planet while the human costs—including vast poverty, immiseration, racialized extraction, and political upheaval—are devastating. The point is that capitalist progress which promises greater freedom from and control over nature results in ever greater subjection to nature. Human intelligence, rationality, and ingenuity are in the service to markets and profit for a tiny number of people at the expense of the very planet that the system depends upon for its survival. Rationality becomes irrationality.

More narrowly, today we see the logic of Enlightenment rationality transform into irrationalism in a number of ways in the realm of education. The logic of testing, the uses of educational technology, and the uses of drugs for education exemplify this. Efforts to improve schooling by applying rational metrics to measure and control it have resulted in forms of teaching that are at odds with learning. The quantification of all educational progress has resulted in teaching to the test at the expense of dialog, thought, and intellectual engagement. The standardization of knowledge results in a prohibition on engaging with key questions as to what knowledge matters, and how claims to truth relate to the interests, ideologies, and social positions of the claimant. Under the rubric of progress and development, education becomes indoctrination and a prohibition on thinking. The uses of educational technologies, including screens and drugs, purport to enhance education; yet, as prior chapters have shown, these instruments of control are largely in the service of anti-intellectual transmission models of pedagogy. These tools that aim for greater and greater mastery and control of the self, nature, and society result in a population whose agency has been undermined as knowledge can only be conceived statically and transactionally rather than in a dynamic manner. Knowledge in contemporary dominant approaches to educational reform serves not enlightenment as self and social understanding or rational progress of humanity and nature but rather control in the service of irrationalism and collective forms of submission and self-destruction such as capitalist, religious, and political fundamentalism.

The use of drugs and screens in education exemplifies the dialectic of Enlightenment's transformation of rationality into irrationalism as well. Drugs such as amphetamines used for attention and focus in school are the result of the application of scientific advancement over generations that allow for the manipulation of human chemistry, affect, and behavior. The various historical uses of the same drug from stimulating the aggression of soldiers to suppressing diet to facilitating focus and attention for transmission pedagogies have all been expressions of rational science being used for irrational ends. The mechanization of war through the application of industrial science has resulted in greater and greater death and destruction from machine guns to aerial bombardment and nuclear weapons. Scientific efficiencies in the mastery of nature produce nature-destroying and potentially world-ending catastrophe. The use of pharmaceuticals for diet is only the consequence of the application of industrial science to food production and the maximization of profit through excess volume of food and the use of food science to make more and more processed, unhealthy, and environmentally destructive food that is mass marketed via the science of marketing manipulation.[3] The focus and attention use of amphetamines respond to a crisis of attention in schools in which the standardization and homogenization of knowledge (under a tradition of industrial efficiency) result in curriculum and pedagogical approaches that are decontextualized, meaningless, and stultifying rather than meaningful, culturally relevant, socially engaged, and a source of social agency—hence motivating. Both the drugs and the standards and accountability movement are the consequence of the misapplication of science to education. And yet, do not drugs and screens have the potential to enchant or reenchant a disenchanted world?

Mind-altering drugs such as psychedelics and imaginative screen content can offer alternative ways of seeing and open questions about the taken for granted experience of the everyday. Enchantment's objects elude rational explanation: mystery, inexplicable phenomena. Such mysterious and unknown things are confronted badly with the recipe of Enlightenment rationality that aims to make the unknown into the known by commonly reducing experience to numbers. These moves may provide a distorted and disengenuous guise of explanatory power. For example, standardized testing as the measure and aim of schooling produces a selective representation of learning that is commonly mis-framed as learning itself. Teaching is then reformed to increase the metrics through, for example, teacher deskilling and routinization rather than toward better aims such as culturally and socially engaged forms of learning fostered by dialog and collaborative investigation.

Enchantment can be conceived of as wonderment, excited imagination or curiosity, a state of intoxication responding to what is strange or novel. Of course, young children are enchanted by things about which older children and adults become jaded. Enchantment with the new does not mean that new experience is authentic in the sense of its meaning being guaranteed, fixed, or beyond interpretation. That is, a state of enchantment does not mean that experience is outside of ideology. Frameworks of meaning that children employ to make sense of what they experience are cultural and grounded in language and cultural politics.[4]

Do screens and drugs enchant people, transporting them to imagine alternative and potentially better realities, or are these technologies in fact largely intoxicants that function like Huxley described in *Brave New World*—soma that lulls people into compliance and complicity with their own oppression? Are these instruments that lure people to briefly escape from the real and distressing conditions of their lives such that they consequently seek more escape as a means of adaptation to existing conditions rather than engagement and struggle to change these conditions? The preceding chapters have argued that the use of screens and drugs for stimulation largely serves the interest of capitalist accumulation and social control. As such, they are instruments for accommodating people to the world as it is rather than serving to question, criticize, and imagine better social, political, and economic alternatives. What is more, the technological industries of stimulation and attention capture, fuel, and feed one another. Screen stimulation renders non-screen time boring and banal. Drug stimulation allows people to endure this banality as well as the drudgery of meaningless forms of work.

A key question is how drugs and screens are used to either foster a tendency to open questions about meanings or whether they stimulate and titillate with novel effects to affirm existing sets of meanings and existing social relations. To be clear, drugs, screens, and other cultural products can always be subject to interrogation and critical interpretation. That is, they can be objects of analysis for critical pedagogies. Traditions of cultural studies, critical media literacy, and critical pedagogy have sought to provide analytical concepts for critically viewing representations. This scholarship suggests that representations can be analyzed through ideology critique (studying how narratives and signs produce meanings in particular cultural formations), relating ideology critique to the political economy of mass media (studying how the ownership and control of media production relates to the kinds of meanings that are produced and circulated), and considering how representations are involved in identity formation (studying how representations form points of identification and subject positions with which people identify).[5]

Some cultural products aim to open questions about the relationships between knowledge, power, and the politics of knowledge, highlighting rather than obscuring social relations. Other cultural products aim to shut down questions about these relationships and social relations by affirming existing sets of meanings. However, all cultural products need to be critically engaged. Critical engagement considers not just interpretation of meanings but the relationship between the making of meaning and broader material and symbolic relations of power and authority. Interpretation of meaning through, for example, ideology critique needs to be taken up in relation to question of political economy such as ownership, control, production, and distribution of cultural products and cultural apparatuses, identity and consciousness formation, and the machinery for the processes of identification, the analysis of broader social antagonisms and competing social and political visions, and the dialectical relationship between subjectivity and the objective social world. The promise and possibility of critical education lie in its capacity for enabling comprehension and reconstruction of experience through acts of interpretation that can become the basis for acts of social intervention and transformation.

So, while drugs and screens may enchant people by inspiring wonder and opening questions about what is, a crucial distinction needs to be made between forms of enchantment that largely serve to intoxicate as a means of escape and diversion from oppressive realities and forms of enchantment that largely inspire the radical imagination. This distinction can be comprehended in terms of two competing promises of control found in drug/screen enchantment and the enchantments of critical theory. Drug/screen enchantment promises to temporarily transport the subject away from oppressive reality. As such, it provides an illusory experience of control—an experience of turning off the world. Critical theories including critical pedagogy promise control by enabling tools of understanding the social context and the self and hence enabling a transformed understanding of both private and public problems. Such a transformed understanding becomes the basis to formulate projects to transform the material world with others, intervene in public problems, and engage in ideological and material struggle for justice, equality, and emancipation.

Notes

Chapter 1

1. William I. Robinson, "Global Capitalism and the Restructuring of Education," in *Into the Tempest : Essays on the New Global Capitalism* (Chicago, IL: Haymarket 2019), 143–62.
2. Stephen Metcalf, "Reading between the Lines: The New Education Law Is a Victory for Bush—and for His Corporate Allies," *The Nation*, January 28, 2002, retrieved June 4, 2024, from https://www.thenation.com/article/archive/reading-between-lines/.
3. David Hursh, *The End of Public Schools: The Corporate Reform Agenda to Privatize Education* (New York: Routledge 2015).
4. Hursh, *The End of Public Schools*. I take this up as well in Kenneth J. Saltman, *The Failure of Corporate School Reform* (New York: Routledge 2012). Critics of the neoliberal restructuring of schooling from a critical perspective include Henry Giroux, Michael Apple, Jean Anyon, John Smyth, Antonia Darder, Pauline Lipman, Enora Brown, Peter McLaren, David Gabbard, Angela Valenzuela, Alexander Means, and Graham Slater, among others.
5. Metcalf, "Reading between the Lines," 18–22.
6. Peter Hart, "What No One Said about NCLB Profiteering," *Fairness and Accuracy in Reporting*, April 30, 2012, retrieved June 4, 2024, from https://fair.org/media_criticism/what-no-one-said-about-nclb-profiteering-except-the-people-who-were-saying-it/; Valerie Strauss, "Big Education Firms Spend Millions Lobbying for Pro- Testing Policies," *The Washington Post,* March 30, 2015.
7. Kenneth J. Saltman, *The Edison Schools: Corporate Schooling and the Assault on Public Education* (New York: Routledge 2005).
8. I detail Social Impact Bond schemes in Kenneth J. Saltman, *The Swindle of Innovative Educational Finance* (Minneapolis, MN: University of Minnesota Press 2018).

9   Kenneth J. Saltman, *The Disaster of Resilience: Education, Digital Privatization, and Profiteering* (London: Bloomsbury 2023).
10 Saltman, *The Disaster of Resilience*.
11 Alan Schwarz, *ADHD Nation: Children, Doctors, Big Pharma, and the Making of an American Epidemic* (New York: Simon & Schuster 2016).
12 Alan Schwarz, "The Selling of Attention Deficit Disorder," *The New York Times*, December 15, 2013, A1.
13 Schwarz, *ADHD Nation*.
14 In several books I have criticized neoliberal reformers who include among many other groups and individuals: right-wing think tanks and ideologues supported by them (AEI, Heritage, Hoover, Cato, Manhattan Institute, Fordham Foundation), venture philanthropists (Gates, Walton, Broad, Dell), philanthrocapitalists that put for profits and non-profits under a single limited liability company (Emerson Collective, Omidyar, CZI), for-profit education corporations, technology companies in education, right-wing ideologues, globe-trotting consultancies (McKinsey, Boston Consulting), education investors (New Schools Venture Fund), investment banks devising innovative privatization schemes (Goldman Sachs), corporate foundations and universities that set up social impact bond privatization schemes, investors in charter school real estate schemes, the voucher, charter, and scholarship tax credit movements.
15 *60 Minutes*, "Boosting Brain Power," April 25, 2010.
16 Alan Schwarz, "Drowned in a Stream of Prescriptions," *The New York Times*, February 2, 2013.
17 A number of both documentary and dramatic films have recently detailed the ways that Perdue Pharma aggressively promoted the mass sales of opioid painkiller oxcontin despite knowing how extremely addictive it is. See, for example, *Pain Killer* (2023), *All the Beauty and the Bloodshed* (2022), *Dopesick* (2021), *The Crime of the Century* (2021).
18 Henry Giroux, *Pedadgogy of Resistance: Against Manufactured Ignorance* (London: Bloomsbury 2022).
19 Brad Evans [interview of Henry Giroux], "Histories of Violence: Life in Zones of Abadonment: A Time to Break the Spectacle of Ignorance and Violence," *LA Review of Books*, August 5, 2019.

20 Herbert Kliebard, *The Struggle for the American Curriculum, 1893–1958* (New York: Taylor & Francis 2004).
21 Paulo Freire, *Pedagogy of the Oppressed* (London: Bloomsbury 2016).
22 Stuart Hall, *Cultural Studies 1983: A Theoretical History* (Durham, NC: Duke University Press 2016). In *Cultural Studies 1983,* Stuart Hall writes, "The notion that one can understand history as a series of rip-offs, by various fractions of the capitalist class, of various fractions of the working class, receives only scorn from Gramsci; it has nothing to do with the processes by which a mode of production reproduces itself."(159)
23 Rachael Zimlich, "Teenagers Plus Heavy Screen Time Equals ADHD?" *Contemporary Pediatrics*, October 2018;35(10):36–7; Chaelin K. Ra, Junhan Cho, Matthew D. Stone, Julianne De La Cerda, Nicholas I. Goldenson, Elizabeth Moroney, Irene Tung, Steve S. Lee, and Adam M. Leventhal, "Association of Digital Media Use with Subsequent Symptoms of Attentiondeficit/ Hyperactivity Disorder among Adolescents," *JAMA,* 2018;320(3):255–63.
24 Jonathan Crary, *Scorched Earth: Beyond the Digital Age to a Post-Capitalist World* (New York: Verso 2022).
25 Franco Berardi, *The Soul at Work: From Alienation to Autonomy* (New York: Semiotext[e] 2009); Franco Berardi, *And: Phenomenology of the End* (New York: Semiotext[e] 2015). Franco Berardi contends that informational flows overwhelm subjectivity resulting in ADHD and pathological states including anxiety, depression, and ADHD.
26 Jonathan Crary, *Suspensions of Perception: Attention, Spectacle, and Modern Culture* (Cambridge: MIT Press 2001), 37.
27 Henry A. Giroux has been making this argument throughout his oeuvre. See, for example, *On Critical Pedagogy, 2nd Edition* (London: Bloomsbury 2020).
28 Theodor Adorno, *History and Freedom* (London: Polity Press 2006), 40.
29 Theodor Adorno, *Introduction to Sociology* (Stanford, CA: Stanford University Press 2000), 32.
30 Adorno, *History and Freedom*, 40.

31 See Eric Gutstein and Bob Peterson (eds.) *Rethinking Mathematics: Teaching Social Justice by the Numbers* (Milwaukee, WI: Rethinking Schools 2013).
32 See Gutstein and Peterson (eds.) *Rethinking Mathematics*.
33 Berardi, *And*, 45–6.
34 Schwarz, "The Selling of Attention Deficit Disorder," A1.
35 CDC, "Facts about ADHD" retrieved October 22, 2023, from https://www.cdc.gov/ncbddd/adhd/data.html.
36 Schwarz, "The Selling of Attention Deficit Disorder," A1.
37 Schwarz, "The Selling of Attention Deficit Disorder," A1.
38 Michael McCarthy, "ADHD Drug Makers Move to Expand into Adult Market," *BMJ*, December 17, 2013; Schwarz, "The Selling of Attention Deficit Disorder," A1.
39 Sam Goldstein, "The Marketing of ADHD," *Annals of the American Psychotherapy Association*, Summer 2000;9(2):32–3.
40 Schwarz, "The Selling of Attention Deficit Disorder," A1.
41 Schwarz, "The Selling of Attention Deficit Disorder," A1.
42 Insights 10, "US ADHD Drugs Market Analysis" insights10.com.
43 Schwarz, "The Selling of Attention Deficit Disorder," A1.
44 Schwarz, *ADHD Nation*, 1–50.
45 Alan Schwarz, "ADHD: The Statistics of a National Disaster," *Significance*, December 2016;13(6):7.
46 Schwarz, "The Selling of Attention Deficit Disorder," 2.
47 Samuele Cortese, Minjin Song, Luis C Farhat, Dong Keon Yon, Seung Won Lee, Min Seo Kim, Seoyeon Park, Jae Won Oh, San Lee, Keun-Ah Cheon, Lee Smith, Corentin J. Gosling, Guilherme V. Polanczyk, Henrik Larsson, Luis A. Rohde, Stephen V. Faraone, Ai Koyanagi, Elena Dragioti, Joaquim Radua, Andre F. Carvalho, Jae Il Shin, and Marco Solmi, "Incidence, Prevalence, and Global Burden of ADHD from 1990 to 2019 across 204 Countries: Data, with Critical Re-analysis, from the Global Burden of Disease Study," *Mol Psychiatry*, 2023;28(11):4823–30. https://doi.org/10.1038/s41380-023-02228-3.
48 Crary, *Suspensions of Perception*, 44.
49 Crary, *Suspensions of Perception*, 4.
50 Crary, *Suspensions of Perception*, 13.

51 Crary, *Suspensions of Perception*, 30.
52 Crary, *Suspensions of Perception*, 31.
53 Crary, *Suspensions of Perception*, 30.
54 Crary, *Suspensions of Perception*, 30.
55 Crary, *Suspensions of Perception*, 35.
56 Nancy Fraser, "From Discipline to Flexibilization: Rereading Foucault in Light of Globalization," *Constellations*, 2003;10(2): 160–71.
57 Samuel Bowles and Herbert Gintis, *Schooling in Capitalist America: Educational Reform and the Contradictions of Economic Life* (Chicago, IL: Haymarket Press 2011 [1976]). Louis Althusser, "Ideology and Ideological State Apparatuses: Notes toward an Investigation," in *Lenin and Philosophy and Other Essays* (New York: Monthly Review Press 1971), 121–76.
58 Robinson, "Global Capitalism and the Restructuring of Education," 143–62.
59 Robinson, "Global Capitalism and the Restructuring of Education," 143–62.
60 Alexander Means, *Learning to Save the Future: Rethinking Education and Work in an Era of Digital Capitalism* (New York: Routledge 2018); Stanley Aronowitz and William Difazio, *The Jobless Future* (Minneapolis, MN: University of Minnesota 1994).
61 Zoe Kleinman, "Elon Musk Tells Rishi Sunak That AI Will Put an End to Work," *BBC*, November 3, 2023, retrieved June 7, 2024, from https://www.bbc.com/news/uk-67302048.
62 Robinson, "Global Capitalism and the Restructuring of Education," 143–62. Nick Couldry and Ulises Meijas, *The Costs of Connection: How Data Is Colonizing Human Life and Appropriating It for Capitalism* (Stanford, CA: Stanford University Press 2019).
63 Jathan Sadowski, "When Data Is Capital: Datafication, Accumulation, and Extraction," *Big Data and Society,* January–June 2019;6:1–12.
64 Ben Williamson and Nelli Piattoeva, "Objectivity as Standardization in Data-Scientific Education Policy, Technology, and Governance," *Learning Media and Technology*, 2019;44(1):64–76.
65 Nancy Fraser, *Cannibal Capitalism* (New York: Verso 2022), 10.
66 I take up these schemes in Saltman, *The Swindle of Innovative Educational Finance* and Saltman, *The Disaster of Resilience*.

67 Fraser, *Cannibal Capitalism*, 2. "Glutton for Punishment: Why Capitalism Is Structurally Racist," 27–52.
68 Fraser, *Cannibal Capitalism*, 20–1.
69 Berardi, *And*, 43.
70 Berardi, *And*, 42.
71 Berardi, *And*, 43.
72 Berardi, *And*, 44.
73 Berardi, *And*, 45.
74 Berardi, *And*, 303.

Chapter 2

1 https://www.calm.com/blog/social-media-and-screen-addiction.
2 Andrea Kane, "How Much Screen Time Is Too Much? The Signs You're Addicted to Your Phone," February 24, 2023, retrieved July 28, 2024, from https://www.cnn.com/2023/02/24/health/screen-time-gupta-podcast-wellness/index.html.
3 Andrea Petersen, "Is Your Child a Digital Addict? Here's What You Can Do," *The New York Times*, April 15, 2020, retrieved July 28, 2024, from https://www.nytimes.com/2020/04/15/parenting/big-kid/child-screen-addiction.html.
4 Council on Communications and Media, David Hill, Nusheen Ameenuddin, Yolanda (Linda) Reid Chassiakos, Corinn Cross, Jeffrey Hutchinson, Alanna Levine, Rhea Boyd, Robert Mendelson, Megan Moreno, and Wendy Sue Swanson, "Media and Young Minds," *Pediatrics,* November 1, 2016;138(5):1–6.
5 Jessica Grose, "Screens Are Everywhere in Schools: Do They Actually Help Kids Learn?" *The New York Times*, March 27, 2024.
6 The concern with screen time undermining self-regulation can be found in popular and scientific discourse as exemplified by a CNN story covering research from the *Journal of the American Medical Association*: Madeline Holcombe, "Giving Your Child a Screen May Hinder Emotional Regulation Study Says: Here's What to Do Instead," *CNN*, December 12, 2022, retrieved July 31, 2024, from https://www.

cnn.com/2022/12/12/health/tantrum-distraction-screens-parenting-wellness/index.html.

7   See Grandview Research's report, "Education Technology Market Size, Share & Trends Analysis Report by Sector," retrieved August 12, 2024, from https://www.grandviewresearch.com/industry-analysis/education-technology-market#:~:text=The%20global%20education%20technology%20market,and%20enhance%20students'%20education%20outcomes. See also The World Economic Forum report, "These Five Key Trends Will Reshape the Edtech Market by 2030," retrieved August 12, 2024, from https://www.weforum.org/agenda/2024/02/these-are-the-4-key-trends-that-will-shape-the-edtech-market-into-2030/.

8   Christina Cipriano, Michael J. Strambler, Lauren H. Naples, Cheyeon Ha, Megan Kirk, Miranda Wood, Kaveri Sehgal, Almut K. Zieher, Abigail Eveleigh, Michael McCarthy, Melissa Funaro, Annett Ponnock, Jason C. Chow, and Joseph Durlak, "The State of Evidence for Social and Emotional Learning: A Contemporary Meta-Analysis of Universal School-Based SEL Interventions," *Child Development*, 2023;94(5):1181–204.

9   I discuss this at length in Saltman, *The Disaster of Resilience*.

10 Saeid Sadeghi, Hikaru Takeuchi, Bita Shalani, Yasuyuki Taki, Rui Nouchi, Ryoichi Yokoyama, Yuka Kotozaki, Seishu Nakagawa, Atsushi Sekiguchi, Kunio Iizuka, Sugiko Hanawa, Tsuyoshi Araki, Carlos Makoto Miyauchi, Kohei Sakaki, Takayuki Nozawa, Shigeyuki Ikeda, Susumu Yokota, Daniele Magistro, Yuko Sassa, and Ryuta Kawashima, "Brain Structures and Activity during a Working Memory Task Associated with Internet Addiction Tendency in Young Adults: A Large Sample Study," *PLOS One*, 2021;16(11):e0259259. https://doi.org/10.1371/journal.pone.0259259; Robert S. Tokunaga, "A Meta-Analysis of Relationships between Psychosocial Problems and Internet Habits: Synthesizing Internet Addiction, Problematic Internet Use, and Deficient Self-Regulation Research," *Communications Monographs*, 2017;84(4):423–46.

11 Positivism posits a false objectivity by concealing the social positions and ideologies of subjects claiming objective, disinterested, and neutral knowledge. For example, standardized tests hide the particular assumptions, values, ideologies, and interests of those who select the

particular knowledge and range of answers that the tests frame as universal. The standards and accountability movement has no use for that which is meaningful and relevant to students and it does not relate knowledge to students' particular lives and experience. It denies the cultural politics of knowledge—that is, the contests over whose knowledge matters and how claims to truth relate to the social positions, interests, and ideologies of the claimants. On "banking education," see Freire, *Pedagogy of the Oppressed*, 75, 82–3.

12 Shu-Yu Kuo, Yu-Ting Chen, Yu-Kai Chang, Pi-Hsia Lee, Mei-Ju Liu, Su-Ru Chen, "Influence of Internet Addiction on Executive Function and Learning Attention in Taiwanese School-Aged Children," *Perspect Psychiatr Care*, 2018;54 (4):495–500; Masaya Morita, Shuntaro Ando, Tomoki Kiyono, Ryo Morishima, Tomoko Yagi, Sho Kanata, Shinya Fujikawa, Syudo Yamasaki, Atsushi Nishida, and Kiyoto Kasai, "Bidirectional Relationship of Problematic Internet Use with Hyperactivity/Inattention and Depressive Symptoms," *Adolescents: A Population-Based Cohort Study European Child & Adolescent Psychiatry*, 2022;31(10):1601–9; Bing-qian Wang, Nan-qi Yao, Xiang Zhou, Jian Liu, and Zheng-tao Lv, "The Association between Attention Deficit/ Hyperactivity Disorder and Internet Addiction: A Systematic Review and Metaanalysis," *BMC Psychiatry*, 2017;17(1):260; Zimlich, "Teenagers Plus Heavy Screen Time Equals ADHD?" 36–7; C. K. Ra, J. Cho, Stone, et al., "Association of Digital Media Use with Subsequent Symptoms of Attentiondeficit/Hyperactivity Disorder among Adolescents," 255–63.

13 Rupesh Enagandula, Shipra Singh, Gaurav W. Adgaonkar, Alka A. Subramanyam, and Ravindra M. Kamath, "Study of Internet Addiction in Children with Attention-Deficit Hyperactivity Disorder and Normal Control," *Industrial Psychiatry Journal*, 2018;27(1):110–14; Maria Panagiotidi and Paul Overton, "Attention Deficit Hyperactivity Symptoms Predict Problematic Mobile Phone Use," *Current Psychology*, 2022;41:2765–71.

14 Morita, et al., "Bidirectional Relationship of Problematic Internet Use with Hyperactivity/Inattention and Depressive Symptoms in Adolescents," 1601–9.

15 Michela Balconi, Irene Venturella, and Roberta Finocchiaro, "Evidences from Rewarding System, FRN and P300 Effect in Internet-addiction in Young People" (SHORT TITLE: Rewarding System and EEG in InternetaAddiction), *Brain Sciences*, 2017;7(7):81; Sadeghi, et al., "Brain Structures and Activity during a Working Memory Task Associated with Internet Addiction Tendency in Young Adults."
16 Schwarz, *ADHD Nation*, 1–50.
17 Stuart Hall's scholarship has been utterly foundational to such scholarship and Henry Giroux stands as an unparalleled theorist of the relationship between media and critical education.
18 William James, *Principles of Psychology* (New York: Holt 1890); Crary, *Scrorched Earth*, 97.
19 Crary, *Scorched Earth*, 40.
20 Crary, *Scorched Earth*, 40.
21 Crary, *Scorched Earth*, 42. Crary's view is preferable to Bernard Stiegler's admonition that the threat posed by digital technology is that it usurps parental authority. Stiegler presumes that the development of thinking in youth depends upon identification with authority rather than wonderment and disidentification explained as well by Erich Fromm who locates the development of rationality with the child's "no" to the parent. See Bernard Stiegler, *Taking Care of Youth and the Generations* (Stanford, CA: Stanford University Press 2008) and Erich Fromm, *Escape from Freedom* (New York: Holt 1994 [original 1941]).
22 Crary, *Scorched Earth*, 42.
23 Crary, *Scorched Earth*, 108.
24 Crary, *Scorched Earth*, 21.
25 Slavoj Zizek, *First as Tragedy, Then as Farce* (New York: Verso 2009).
26 Zygmunt Bauman, *In Search of Politics* (Cambridge: Polity 1999).
27 Kenneth J. Saltman, "The Strong Arm of the Law," *Cultural Politics*, 2003;9(4):49–67; Kenneth J. Saltman, *The Alienation of Fact: Digital Educational Privatization, AI, and the False Promise of Bodies and Numbers* (New York: Routledge 2022).
28 Franco Berardi, *Heroes: Mass Murder and Suicide* (New York: Verso 2015).
29 Erika Edwards and Hallie Jackson, "Social Media Is Driving Teen Mental Health Crisis, Surgeon General Warns," *NBC News*, November 23, 2023.

30   Franco "Bifo" Berardi, *And: Phenomenology of the End* (Los Angeles: Semiotext(e) 2015), 48.
31   Bifo, *And*, 190.
32   Zygmunt Bauman, *Consuming Life* (Cambridge: Polity 2007).
33   Jamie Manolev, Anna Sullivan, and Roger Slee, "The Datafication of Discipline: Class Dojo, Surveillance, and a Performative Classroom Culture," *Learning Media and Technology*, December 14, 2018:1–16.
34   Michel Foucault, *Discipline and Punish: The Birth of the Prison* (New York: Vintage 1977).
35   Henry Giroux, "Educators as Public Intellectuals and the Challenge of Fascism," *Policy Futures in Education,* 2024;0(0):1–7. Giroux draws on C. Wright Mills's call for translation of private into public problems and suggests that educators as public intellectuals need to foster this capacity in students.
36   Crary, *Scorched Earth*, 99–100.

Chapter 3

1   Pen America, "Educational Censorship" https://pen.org/issue/educational-censorship/.
2   Peter Wade, Patrick Reis, "CPAC Speaker Calls for Eradication of 'Transgenderism'—and Somehow Claims He Is Not Calling for Elimination of Transgender People," *Rolling Stone,* March 6, 2023, retrieved April 1, 2024, https://www.rollingstone.com/politics/politics-news/cpac-speaker-transgender-people-eradicated-1234690924/.
3   Judith Butler, *Who's Afraid of Gender?* (New York: Farrar, Straus, and Giroux, 2024).
4   The rise of contemporary fascism has been taken up by a number of contemporary scholars including the late Sheldon Wolin in his important book *Democracy, Inc*. Henry Giroux has been both a major public intellectual warning of the rise of fascism and one of few who has long linked it to education. Jason Stanley, Timothy Snyder, and Alberto Toscano have made important recent contributions to analyzing the resurgence and distinctiveness of fascism now.

5   CPAC 2024 cite.
6   Nancy Fraser, *The Old Is Dying and the New Cannot Be Born: From Progressive Neoliberalism to Trumpism and Beyond* (New York: Verso 2019).
7   Robin Truth Goodman, *Gender Commodity: Marketing Feminist Identities and the Promise of Security* (New York: Bloomsbury 2022), 129.
8   Spencer Kornhaber, "Trump's Plan to Police Gender," *The Atlantic*, December 7, 2023 and Sonali Kolhatkar, "Why Republicans Are Betting the Farm on Attacking Transgender People," *Counterpunch*, April 12, 2021.
9   Paul B. Preciado, *Testo-Junkie: Sex, Drugs, and Politics in the Pharmacopornographic Era* (New York: Feminist Press 2013).
10 Goodman, *Gender Commodity* explores the relationship between the reproduction of capitalism and the reproduction of gender including transgender identity.
11 Fraser, *The Old Is Dying and the New Cannot Be Born*.
12 Michel Foucault, *The History of Sexuality*, Volume I (New York: Vintage 1977); Judith Butler, *Gender Trouble: Feminism and the Subversion of Identity* (New York: Routledge 1990); Judith Butler, *Bodies That Matter: On the Discursive Limits of "Sex"* (New York: Routledge 1993); Judith Butler, *Undoing Gender* (New York: Routledge 2004); Preciado, *Testo-Junkie*.
13 Butler, *Gender Trouble*.
14 Butler, *Bodies That Matter*, 126.
15 Butler, *Bodies That Matter*, 125.
16 Althusser, "Ideology and Ideological State," 121–76. Althusser's conception of ideology as subject formation or "interpellation" describes a process of the subject being hailed by the Subject of authority (teacher, cop, etc.) and in turning the subject is both recognized by the Subject and recognizes herself. Althusser importantly links ideological subject formation to the ideology producing institutions and the repressive institutions providing an account of how the social order and capitalism are reproduced by recreating the social relationships necessary for the maintenance of the

order. Among the limitations of Althusser's model of subject formation is a limited conception of how consciousness and particularly critical consciousness and resistance can be cultivated through educational practices. See Henry A. Giroux's *Theory and Resistance in Education: Towards a Pedagogy for the Opposition* (London: Bloomsbury 2024) for a thorough discussion of Althusser's model in the context of other social and cultural reproduction theorists.
17 Gilles Deleuze and Felix Guatarri, *Anti-Oedipus: Capitalism and Schizophrenia* (Minneapolis, MN: University of Minnesota Press 1972).
18 The Editorial Board of the Kansas City Star, "Questioning Josh Hawley's Sexuality Is Not OK, Even if It Is Josh Hawley," *The Kansas City Star*, November 10, 2021.
19 Preciado, *Testo-Junkie*, 163.
20 Preciado, *Testo-Junkie*, 205.
21 Sadowski, "When Data Is Capital," 1–12.
22 Williamson and Piattoeva, "Objectivity as Standardization," 64–76.
23 Noah DeLissovoy, Alexander Means, and Kenneth J. Saltman, *Toward a New Common School Movement* (New York: Routledge 2014).
24 Ann Arnett Ferguson, *Bad Boys: Public Schooling in the Making of Black Masculinity* (Ann Arbor, MI: University of Michigan Press 2001).
25 Preciado, *Testo-Junkie*, 371–2.
26 Preciado, *Testo-Junkie*, 378.

Chapter 4

1 https://www.nbcnews.com/health/health-news/anxiety-medication-therapy-children-teens-study-rcna87874.
2 https://www.cdc.gov/childrensmentalhealth/features/anxiety-depression-children.html.
3 https://www.cdc.gov/childrensmentalhealth/features/anxiety-depression-children.html.
4 https://childmind.org/article/medications-for-anxiety-in-children/#antidepressants.

5   https://www.nbcnews.com/health/health-news/anxiety-medication-therapy-children-teens-study-rcna87874; https://childmind.org/article/medications-for-anxiety-in-children/.
6   Fortune Business Insights, "Anxiety Disorders and Depression Treatment Market Size, Share & Covid-19 Impact Analysis," June 17, 2024, retrieved July 3, 2024, from https://www.fortunebusinessinsights.com/anxiety-and-depression-treatment-market-102787.
7   William I. Robinson, *Global Civil War: Capitalism Post-Pandemic* (Oakland, CA: PM Press 2022), 3.
8   Robinson, *Global Civil War*, 38.
9   Bauman, *In Search of Politics*.
10 Fraser, "From Discipline to Flexibilization," 160–71; Zygmunt Bauman *Globalization: The Human Consequences* (New York: Columbia University Press 1998).
11 Giroux, *Theory and Resistance in Education*.
12 Robert W. McChesney, *The Problem of the Media: U.S. Communication Politics in the 21st Century* (New York: Monthly Review Press 2004).
13 Martin Gilens and Benjamin Page, "Testing Theories of American Politics: Elites, Interest Groups, and Average Citizens," *Perspectives on Politics*, September 18, 2014;12(3):564–81.
14 Ellen Barry, "Surgeon General Calls for Warning Labels on Social Media Platforms," *The New York Times*, June 17, 2024; Kira E. Riehm, Kenneth A. Feder, Kayla N. Tormohlen, Rosa M. Crum, Andrea S. Young, Kerry M. Green, Lauren R. Pacek, Lareina N. La Flair, and Ramin Mojtabai, "Associations between Time Spent Using Social Media and Internalizing and Externalizing Problems among US Youth," *JAMA Psychiatry*, 2019;76(12):1266–73. https://doi.org/10.1001/jamapsychiatry.2019.2325.
15 Berardi, *And*, 42.
16 Berardi, *And*, 42.
17 Jonathan Crary, *24/7: Late Capitalism and the Ends of Sleep* (New York: Verso 2013).
18 Berardi, *And*, 44.
19 Byun Chul Han, *The Burnout Society* (Stanford, CA: Stanford University Press 2015).

20 Michel Foucault, *Discipline and Punish: The Birth of the Prison* (New York: Vintage 1975).
21 Pierre Bourdieu, "The Forms of Capital," in J. Richardson (Ed.) *Handbook of Theory and Research for the Sociology of Education* (New York: Greenwood 1986), 105–18.
22 Theodor W. Adorno, *Introduction to Sociology* (Stanford, CA: Stanford University Press 2000); Theodor W. Adorno, *Lectures on Negative Dialectics: Fragments of a Lecture Course 1965/1966* (Malden, MA: Polity 2008); Henry A. Giroux, *Theory and Resistance in Education*.
23 Edwards and Jackson "Social Media Is Driving Teen Mental Health Crisis, Surgeon General Warns."
24 https://jamanetwork.com/journals/jamapsychiatry/fullarticle/2749480.
25 Paul Tough, *How Children Succeed: Grit, Curiosity, and the Hidden Power of Character* (New York: Houghton-Mifflin 2012).
26 Bourdieu, "The Forms of Capital," 241–8.
27 Vincent J. Felitti, Robert F. Anda, Dale Nordenberg, David F. Williamson, Alison M. Spitz, Valerie Edwards, Mary P. Koss, and James S. Marks, "Relationship of Childhood Abuse and Household Dysfunction to Many of the Leading Causes of Death in Adults: The Adverse Childhood Experiences (ACE) Study," *American Journal of Preventive Medicine*, 1998;14(4):245–58.
28 Lego Foundation site on migrants and trauma. https://equity-ed.net/reimagining-childhood-through-playful-learning-for-800000-refugees-in-east-africa/; See also Saltman, *The Alienation of Fact*, 4. "The Lego Foundation and the Quantification of Play."
29 C. Wright Mills, *The Sociological Imagination* (Oxford: Oxford University Press 1959).

Chapter 5

1 Michael Pollan, *How to Change Your Mind: The New Science of Psychedelics* (New York: Penguin 2019).
2 Pollan, *How to Change Your Mind*, 304.

3 *How to Change Your Mind* (film). Michael Pollan interviews neuroscientist Robin Carhardt-Harris in both the film and book. In the book, see "Chapter 5: The Neuroscience: Your Brain on Psychedelics" and more specifically page 313.
4 Pollan, *How to Change Your Mind*, 313–14.
5 DemocracyNow!, "Noam Chomsky on How Businesses Sought to Destroy the Democratic Movements of the 60's," April 5, 2017, retrieved July 25, 2024, from https://www.democracynow.org/2017/4/5/noam_chomsky_on_how_businesses_sought.
6 Christian Parenti, *Lockdown America: Police and Prisons in the Age of Crisis* (New York: Verso 2008). See also, Michelle Alexander, *The New Jim Crow: Mass Incarceration in the Age of Colorblindness* (New York: The New Press 2010) and Loic Wacquant, *Punishing the Poor: The Neoliberal Government of Social Insecurity* (Durham, NC: Duke University Press 2009).
7 https://www.nbcnews.com/meet-the-press/data-download/costs-war-drugs-continue-soar-rcna92032.
8 The documentary film *All the Beauty and the Bloodshed* provides a powerful account of the success of activists and artists to hold the Sacklers and Purdue Pharma accountable and to get the Sackler name removed from museums. The film centers on photographer and activist Nan Goldin.
9 https://www.aclu.org/sites/default/files/infographics/090116-sttp-graphic.jpg.
10 https://www.publichealth.columbia.edu/profile/seth-prins-phd.
11 United States Sentencing Commission, "Demographic Differences in Federal Sentencing" November 2023 (2017–2021) https://www.ussc.gov/sites/default/files/pdf/research-and-publications/research-publications/2023/20231114_Demographic-Differences.pdf.
12 William I. Robinson, *Into the Tempest: Essays on the New Global Capitalism* (Chicago, IL: Haymarket 2019).
13 Sharon Zhang, "Major Brands Like McDonald's, Kroger, and Coca-Cola Linked to Forced Labor," *Truthout*, January 30, 2024, retrieved from https://truthout.org/articles/major-brands-like-mcdonalds-

kroger-and-coca-cola-linked-to-forced-prison-labor/#:~:text=A%20sprawling%20new%20investigation%20has,%2C%20Coca%2DCola%20and%20Kroger.
14 Fraser, *Cannibal Capitalism*, 1–28.
15 Fraser, *Cannibal Capitalism*, 29–40.
16 Democracy Now, "Ahead of Juneteenth, Maryland Pardons 175k Pot Convictions, Seeking to Remedy Harm of War on Drugs," June 18, 2024.

Conclusion

1 Max Weber, *The Protestant Ethic and the Spirit of Capitalism* (New York: Scribner 1958); Max Horkheimer and Theodor Adorno, *Dialectic of Enlightenment* (New York: Continuum 1944).
2 Horkheimer and Adorno, *Dialectic of Enlightenment*, 3–42.
3 See Eric Schlosser, *Fast Food Nation: The Dark Side of the All-American Meal* (New York: Houghton-Mifflin 2001).
4 Debra Van Ausdale and Joe Feagin's, *The First R: How Children Learn Race and Racism* (Lanham, MD: Rowman & Littlefield 2001) illustrates how young children use racial ideologies that they have learned from the culture in their play.
5 See Stuart Hall, *Representation: Cultural Representations and Signifying Practices* (Thousand Oaks, CA: Sage 1997).

Index

adaptive and non-adaptive strategies 90–1
Adderall (drug) 7, 16, 22, 35, 64
addictive stimulation 35–44
Adorno, Theodor W.
  Dialectic of Enlightenment 49–50, 118–19
  "the essentially real" 13, 40, 49, 118–19
Adverse Childhood Experiences (ACEs) 89
Althusser, Louis 135–6 n.16
American Civil Liberties Union 106
American Psychological Association 6, 31
Amira Learning 20, 46
amphetamine (drug) 7, 10, 16–17, 22, 27–8, 111, 120–1
anxiety 56, 59, 78–86
artificial intelligence (AI) 5, 21, 25
  AI avatars in schools 50, 66
Attention Deficit Hyperactivity Disorder (ADHD) 1, 5–8, 10, 12, 14–18, 27–9, 33–7, 111
authoritarian movement 41, 56

banking education 9, 12, 33, 88
Bashant, Jennifer, *Building a Trauma-informed Compassionate Classroom* 89–91
Bauman, Zygmunt
  politics 80
  "subjectivity fetishism" in *Consuming Life* 43–4
Berardi, Franco 14–15, 28, 40, 82, 127 n.25
  Heroes 42
  The Soul at Work, Heroes, and *And* 26–7

biocodes of gender 68–76
bio-communism 62
biological stimulation 9
Bourdieu, Pierre 84, 87
Brown, Anthony 113–14
Browning, Robert, "The Pied Piper of Hamlin" 37
Butler, Judith, performative theory 58–60, 73

cannabis (drug) 100, 104, 106, 108, 113–14
capitalism 20, 23–6, 70, 119
  financialized 21, 23–4, 108, 110–11
  industrial 18–19, 108
  racial 113–14
capitalist enclosure 70
Carhart-Harris, Kevin 102
Center for Disease Control (CDC) 15–16, 78–9
charter schools 3–5, 94
Chicago Boys group 87
Christianity 54–5
Class Dojo app 20, 44–6, 93
commons 68–70, 72–3, 75–6
Conners, Keith 17
Conservative Political Action Conference (CPAC) 53–4
contemporary fascism 134 n.4
Covid-19 pandemic 31–2, 79, 109
Crary, Jonathan 11, 18–19, 28, 39–41, 51, 133 n.21
criminalization 105–7, 113, 117
critical education 8, 116, 118, 123
critical pedagogy 39, 51–2, 76, 78, 91, 95–7, 112–13, 116–18, 123–4
critical social theory 112–13
cultural capital 84, 87

cybertime and cyberspace 27
cyber utopianism 42–3

decriminalization 107–8
Democratic Party (United States) 80
digital resilience products 44–9, 77, 94
digital resilience programs 34–5, 44, 78, 89
direct coercion 19–20
disenchantment, digital 34–44, 83, 118
drag king workshops 73–4
drug attention education complex, conditions for 2–15
drugging children 7, 12–13, 15–18, 29
drug legalization 99–104, 107, 110–12
drug stimulation 36, 64, 69, 122

Educational Management Organizations 4–5
educational technology 32, 34, 50, 84–5, 119–20
Elementary and Secondary Education Act (ESEA) 3
enchantment 37–8, 116, 121–2, 124
enlightenment rationality 49–50, 118–19, 121

financialized capitalism 21, 23–4, 108, 110–11
Foucault, Michel 11, 45, 58–60, 84
Fraser, Nancy 28, 54
  Cannibal Capitalism 23–6
  "progressive neoliberal" 57
"freedom" 54–5
Freire, Paulo 9, 38, 88
Freud, Sigmund 77–8

gender 55 6
  critical pedagogies of 73
  difference 56, 59, 69
  performativity 60
  and sexuality 53, 56–63, 68–71

Giroux, Henry A. 8–9, 134 n.4
Go Noodle app 20, 47
Goodman, Robin Truth, *Gender Commodity* 55, 135 n.10
"grooming" children 58

Hall, Stuart 10
Han, Byun Chul 82–3
Hawley, Josh 63
heterosexuality 54, 59–60
Horkheimer, Max, *Dialectic of Enlightenment* 49–50, 118–19
human capital theory 86–8

illicit drugs 1, 101
industrial capitalism 19, 108
International Monetary Fund 88
Internet Complex 39–41

James, William 37

Knowles, Michael, "eradicating transgender identity" 53

labor exploitation 24–5, 81
language learning apps 12–13
Leap Innovations 5
learned self-discipline 19–20, 71, 81
legalization. *See* drug legalization
Lego and the Lego Foundation 22, 67, 94, 138 n.28
Livingston, Jennie, *Paris Is Burning* 59
LSD (psychedelic drug) 101, 103, 110
Lynch, David 92

macrodosing 103, 110
mass incarceration 104, 107–9
microdosing 102–3, 110
Mills, C. Wright 95
Moore, Wesley 113–14
Murthy, Vivek 82
Musk, Elon 21

neoliberal education
  environment 33
  reform 6–9
  restructuring 70–2, 74–5
neoliberal ideology 80
neoliberalism 6, 43
New Schools Venture Fund 5, 94
Nixon, Richard, "War on Drugs" 104
No Child Left Behind Law (NCLB) 2–7

Obetrol (drug) 17
Organization for Economic Collaboration and Development (OECD) 22, 67, 87, 94

Passeron, Jean-Claude 87
passive stimulation of screens 38, 41, 44–9, 52
pharmaceutical stimulants 1, 9, 11, 22, 30, 34, 65
pharmacopornographic technology 65
Pollan, Michael, *How to Change Your Mind* 101–2
pornification of labor 65–6
post-traumatic stress disorder (PTSD), treatment for 110
Preciado, Paul B. 58, 60–3, 65–70, 73–4
privatization, educational 3–5, 9, 23, 26, 71–2, 74–6, 80–1, 94, 109
Prosobiec, Jack 54
psilocybin mushrooms 101
psychedelic drugs 101–4, 108, 110–13, 115, 121
psychiatric talk therapy 19
Purdue Pharma (Sackler family) 100, 105–6

racial capitalism 113–14
racialized incarceration 110–12
right-wing politics 53–8, 60, 80, 82–3
Robinson, William I. 20–2, 28, 108

Saltman, Kenneth J., *The Disaster of Resilience* 45, 89, 94
scapegoating 56, 88
school commercialism 5, 44
school sports 57–8, 69, 71–2, 74
school to prison pipeline 100, 106–9, 113–14, 116
Schwarz, Alan 6, 15–16
screen addiction
  ADHD and 35–7
  crisis of 31, 33–5, 43
  problem of 33–4
  theory of 35–44
screen products 29, 32, 44–5, 48
screen stimulation 36, 64, 122
screen usage by children 8, 10, 29–30, 33–5, 38
Selective Serotonin Norepinephrine Reuptake Inhibitors (SSNRIs) 79
Selective Serotonin Reuptake Inhibitors (SSRIs) 79
self-driving vehicles 21
self-hood 62–3
semio-capitalism 14–15, 26–7, 42–4, 82
Social and Emotional Learning (SEL) 5, 20, 22, 25, 28, 32, 44–8, 50–1, 75, 91–5
social capital 87
social impact bond 5, 23, 126 n.14
social media 32, 39, 42–4, 63, 81–3, 85, 93
social philosophy 112–13
standards and accountability movement 1–4, 27–8, 45–6, 91, 121, 132 n.11

test-based accountability 4, 10
testosterone 53, 58, 61, 69
trans athletes 1, 57, 72
trans identity 55–7
transnational capitalist class (TCC) 20–1

trauma 77-8, 85-6
    to critical pedagogy 95-7
    human capital theory 86-8
    -informed pedagogy 89-91
    and poverty 86
    resilience and treatment 91-5
Trumpism 54, 80

voucher schemes 5

World Bank 88

Zizek, Slavoj 40
Zoo U program 20, 46, 95